COLLEGE SUCCESS HABITS

7 Powerful Principles to Help You Excel in College and Beyond

Jesse Mogle

HybridGlobal
PUBLISHING

Published by
Hybrid Global Publishing
301 East 57th Street
4th Floor
New York, NY 10022

Manufactured in the United States of America, or in the United Kingdom when distributed elsewhere.

Mogle, Jesse
    College Success Habits: 7 Powerful Principles to Help You
    Excel in College and Beyond
LCCN: 2020900548
ISBN: 978-1-951943-03-5
eBook: 978-1-951943-04-2

Cover design by: Joe Potter
Cover photo by: Brooke Ritter Photography
Copyediting and interior design by: Claudia Volkman

www.jessemogle.com

ACKNOWLEDGMENTS

I would like to thank:

Mary Castle Elementary's Mrs. Perkins for being there for a traumatized child who didn't know how to cope with his home life.

Columbus North High School's Mr. Askins (my algebra teacher) for showing me that language was my future and my history professor, Mr. Niespodziani (Nespo) for showing me how much fun learning can be through all the cool lectures you gave with music as the theme—and, of course, all the inspirational quotes on your walls.

University of Florida's one-and-only Master Lecturer Mike Foley for not pushing me out of the Journalism School because it took me three times to pass 101. Sorry I was such a hungover dunderhead.

And absolutely, positively, most importantly, my student adviser, Sandra Storr. I would not have graduated from UF had you not seen something in me that I wasn't able to see for myself until I was in my forties and sober. No one cared more about me and my graduation at that school than you. Thank you for listening to me cry, laugh, and dream big. I am still humbled by your love and support during those five years. My gratitude toward you is unwavering, my love undying.

Matt Brauning and the Evolution community for being such a massive instigator of my personal and professional evolution.

A shout-out to Boo-Boo for being on this ride with me the longest. I love that we got sober together.

And to all my friends and family for loving old Jesse and embracing new Jesse—I love you.

We all live under the same sky,
but we all don't have the same horizon.
KONRAD ADENAUER (VIA MR. NESPO)

TABLE OF CONTENTS

INTRODUCTION

As the freezing air burst across my face and the snow whipped and swirled into my eyes, I was immediately chilled to the bone in a way I had never experienced. The fallen snow, in the gutter, looked like black mud, while along the sidewalk it had been plowed into drifts taller than my head. I was wearing jeans and a t-shirt, and my sneakers were soaked through with icy, cold, sludgy slush. It felt like a thousand needles poking at the bottom of my feet.

Looking back, it's pretty clear that my parents didn't check the weather before we took off. That oversight was just the beginning of the mistakes they made along this journey. This wasn't a vacation—this was our new hell, and it was so far from sunny Orlando that I despised it from day one.

In 1984 my family moved from the sunshine of America's playground—the home of Disney World and Sea World—to the misery that is the Midwestern Winter. My stepdad became a partner and general manager for multiple Budget car sales dealerships in Indianapolis, Indiana, and we were going to suffer for his career ambitions for years to come.

We moved into a Ramada Inn while our realtor found us a house. It was in that crap hole that my mom first showed signs of the illness that had been eating away at her insides for years prior. Shortly after we settled into the inspiration for the Bates Motel, my mother began drinking Pepto-Bismol like it was water.

Her complaints of a stomachache escalated into crying in the bathroom, which further escalated to an ambulance ride to the hospital. Soon after, my sister and I found ourselves alone in the hotel room, day after day, as my dad went to work, and my mother went in and out of the hospital.

After a couple of weeks, we moved into the scary house on Sergeant Road, and Mom checked into the hospital for the entirety of spring and most of the summer.

As a child, I couldn't wrap my head around what the hell had happened. Our 1983 New Year's Eve had included playing with giant Floridian turtles in our backyard, sparklers in hand, as we counted down the ball for 1984. New Year's Day was a festival of finger foods and playing in our hot tub, in what we considered wintery temperatures: the mid-sixtiess.

Here comes June 15th, my ninth birthday, and my sister and I are left clueless as to why Mom can't come home. Grandma came from Oklahoma to stay with us, which exacerbated our fears that Mom wouldn't return to us. All the while, Dad worked twelve to fifteen-hour days at the dealership.

I know the suspense is killing you, so here's the diagnosis: my mom had Crohn's disease. Being the mid-eighties, the knowledge base on Crohn's and colitis was in its infancy. My mother underwent no less than twenty surgeries over the next three years, and she went from a vibrant twenty-nine-year-old to a shell of herself wearing a permanent colostomy bag.

This colostomy bag was the bane of my family's existence from that point on. If you are unfamiliar with this medical device, here is a summary. When you have all your intestines taken out through countless surgeries, you get to go to the bathroom in a bag glued to your hip, and this is your life till you die.

This bag technology was archaic at best, and downright medieval torture at its worst. The bag tended to bust open or leak at the most inopportune times—and any time your bathroom bag opens when you're not in the bathroom is an inopportune time.

The grocery store, department store, airport, zoo, school, kitchen, backyard, my mom and dad's bed—name a place, and it leaked there. Dad's propensity to escape this chaos through long hours at the office left me as the pseudo man of the house. At the age of nine, I took on the responsibility of helping my mom clean up the mess when the bag busted.

I have so many stories from my childhood about bag cleanups that I could write a book about the comedic situations that unraveled when that contraption went bust.

Mom used to say, "If you can't laugh at yourself, who can you laugh at?"

Yeah, I get my dark sense of humor from her.

My barely developed brain had to figure out a way to live in this new world, so I became very formulaic in my activities, studies, and life in general. I turned everything into a process, a sequence—unconscious, habituated actions—so I could control the chaos of our home life as much as possible.

Unbeknownst to me, I was laying the foundation for future habits and behaviors that I still follow today. You, too, have been cultivating habits since you were in diapers, and a majority of the reactions you have to situations now were formed way back then.

When I sobered up for good in 2017, I began a healing journey that was sorely needed since I had been an infant. My environment—from the womb until this moment right now—has influenced the man I've become. The results of the imprinting, implanting, matching, and mirroring that I underwent since conception have shaped everything you will read in this book.

Every one of the seven principles I share in this book became a cornerstone of my childhood. I just wasn't aware of them until I became sober.

My early years were mentally and emotionally draining. My tween and teenage years consisted of us living on a family farm-like plot of land in Columbus, Indiana, and the beaches of Daytona Beach, Florida. Mom's life was a roller coaster of good and bad days, months, years. Dad never stopped working from before sunrise to well after sunset.

When my parents announced their divorce in the summer of 1994, mere months from my freshman year in college . . . well, all hell broke loose.

With Mom back in Florida, Dad working fifteen-hour days in Indianapolis, and my own car and a job, it was the perfect storm for me to get swept up in. Weed on my birthday led to a Grateful Dead acid trip in July, and that led to consistent boozing, which set me up for disaster come the fall semester.

I was a straight-A student in high school, minus Mr. Askins' Algebra 2 class, so my demise into addiction wasn't exactly foreshadowed. My family's genetic history does leave me predisposed to it, but I did not think these intoxicated behaviors were a precursor to a future rocked by addiction.

I was wrong.

I was so wrong.

I might have seen it coming.

I'm not sure.

It was a long time ago.

But this I know: I ignored ALL the key signs that addiction was setting up a permanent camp in my life.

It's like I thought I was invincible!

Nothing could touch me!

Life would work out in my favor no matter what I did!

I was a super-teenager! I was a super twenty-something!

As you can probably surmise, there were a lot of ebbs and flows.

INTRODUCTION

In this book I will talk about some of the stories that led me to you. Others you will have to see me live, on stage, to hear — or subscribe and listen to the College Success Habits podcast, because I certainly overshare there.

I am writing this book for you, the college student, the soon-to-be college student, or the about-to-be-out-of-college, student.

You probably think you have everything under control. You very well might. I am not here to challenge what you have already done. In fact, I am not here to challenge, judge, or otherwise tell you how to live your life.

Instead, I wrote the book I wish I would have read when I started college.

I wrote the book that I would've ignored had someone handed it to me in 1994.

I wrote this book because I know there are hundreds of thousands of young adults graduating into or out of college every year, and most of them have been raised in an emotionally immature environment.

Again, this is not a knock on your parents, your friends, your relatives—or anyone else who has played an integral role in who you have grown to be today—including you yourself.

Our society has a lot of gaps in our education system. Most of all, we are not raised to be self-aware, introspective, or healthily in touch with our emotions.

The power principles I discuss in this book will open your eyes to your habits and behaviors you like about yourself and those you would like to change for the better.

You are in charge of your life now. You are in charge of the person you become from here on out.

Do not let what made you shape you. Meaning: your parents who made you are no longer who will shape you.

You shape you. You can make any choice you want. You can justify any behavior or decision you make. Wouldn't you rather not have to spend so much time justifying your actions to yourself or others?

I believe your mind will find a justification for everything you do and experience.

When people say "Everything happens for a reason," I consider this statement their way of justifying whatever happened to them—a way to put a positive spin on it. Because if things don't happen for a reason, then we would probably see bad things happening to us as a punishment, instead of an experience that gives us feedback to learn from.

Get a bad grade—it happened for a reason.

Get in an accident—it happened for a reason.

Leave a relationship—it happened for a reason.

Hindsight being 20/20 and all, anything that happens can have a conceivable reason when one looks back on it.

I'm not all about that predetermined life stuff.

I do think we have free will to make the choices we make, but I also believe we have unconscious behaviors and habits instilled in us, from the womb on up, that we weren't even aware we absorbed. I think these behaviors and habits direct our lives way more than we realize.

After you read this book, I hope you firmly believe: If you control the vision you have for your life, you will attain it.

A habit is an unconscious behavior or process your brain has memorized so it can use less energy when a trigger instigates the programmed action—**and you choose to live with that habit.**

A trigger is something that activates the habit—for example, an alarm that wakes you up so you get out of bed and brush your teeth.

It can be a conscious habit, such as smoking cigarettes, but the trigger and programming are wired into your unconscious, so even though you know it's terrible for you, you still do it.

You can change any habit if you pull the trigger and

programming into your conscious mind and focus on it until it feels, looks, or sounds the way you want it to.

You are in charge of your life, and your choices are now your responsibility to make and to accept credit or fault.

You are capable of creating a vision and living it—period. I believe this is what it means to be human. I believe this is the meaning of life.

To create a vision for your life and pursue it.

Every.

Single.

Day.

Unfortunately, I allowed addiction to seize me by the throat and drown me for over two decades. I have spent the last three years righting my ship and navigating myself back on course.

I hope by reading this book, you will foresee the negative trappings around you and overcome them with the grace I so clearly lacked for far too many years.

Every day you get to choose the energy you put out to the world. **I think of energy as a moving toward or away from motivation.**

If you move toward something, your energy is positive.

If you move away from something, your energy is negative.

When you study because you want to learn something new to make yourself a better, more well-rounded person, that is a positive, toward energy.

If you study because you are afraid of being a failure, inadequate, or stupid, that is a negative, away-from energy.

This is your chance, right now, to choose to be energetically positive from this day forward. The principles in this book are your road map toward this accomplishment.

The tendency is to fall back on your old patterns and habits—to return to what is comfortable, to keep with tradition.

If you tend only to do something when ordered or told to, then the freedom college allows may seem too much for you to handle. If you tend to challenge authority, then college may seem too structured and rigid for you.

You choose your attitude.
You choose what lens to view life through.
You choose your perspective.
You choose the thoughts you listen to.
You choose the thoughts you ignore.
You choose the feelings you feel.
You choose the feelings you ignore.

Most importantly, realize that every action you take is your choice to make. Whether the results are positive or negative, you don't get to choose to accept responsibility for your actions only when it's convenient. You must accept the congratulations that come when your actions lead to positive outcomes; however, you are not allowed to blame others for your actions that lead to negative outcomes.

Adulthood is tricky. You will witness people you think have it all together do some pretty dumb stuff—and you might think that gives you a pass to do it too.

It does not.

Your parents and relatives were your first teachers. Depending on their habits and behaviors, what you saw and experienced through them could have guided you rightly or off the cliff.

Do not let what made you shape you.

You are in charge of your growth now. Your emotional maturity is more important than your intelligence quotient. Please be diligent in your emotional growth, as it will determine your outcome way more than your intelligence ever will.

Observe everyone around you as part of your life's experiment. Take little pieces from all of them and construct your world as you want it to be. Your vision is your vision until you start letting other voices drown out your own. Then what you want is really just an assortment of what others want for or from you.

Gain the clarity in your vision, the confidence to begin achieving it, and the control necessary to see it through with the seven guiding principles I'll share with you in this book.

Stick with this. If you choose to follow my road map, don't whimsically change road maps three months from now because you haven't won a Nobel prize or purchased your first mega-yacht.

By no means am I deflating my book, but, honestly, almost any self-help book you read will lead you to a positive outcome if you follow its tenets for months and years to come.

If you have the growth mindset that you can accomplish anything, the courage to be decisive and to take action, the discipline to push ahead, the flexibility to overcome obstacles, and the tenacious drive to show up every day and be the best version of yourself—you will achieve everything you prioritize in your life.

No matter what age you are or at what point in your life we are meeting—no matter, no matter, no matter—if you read these principles, adopt them into your life, and keep at it every day, you will be in more control of your journey.

I guarantee it.

Your life's vision is your north star.

It will guide you toward your life's meaning if you keep your focus on it. This book is your navigation map.

I am honored that you are using it.

CHAPTER 1

DEVELOP A GROWTH MINDSET

In a **growth mindset,** *people believe that their most basic abilities can be developed through dedication and hard work—brains and talent are just the starting point. This view creates a love of learning and a resilience that is essential for great accomplishment.*
CAROL S. DWECK

Developing a growth mindset is essential if you want to experience all that life has to offer. It is the first principle because it is the foundation upon which all the other principles are grounded.

A willingness to explore new ideas, new opinions, new information—and being open to all the people who will bring those things to you—will change your life for the better in innumerable ways.

Carol Dweck, professor of psychology at Stanford and author of the book *Mindset: The New Psychology of Success*, categorized mindsets as either growth or fixed.

Having a growth mindset means that you are ready to learn new things whenever presented with them. You believe you can learn new things, and you know your current skills and talents are not the ceiling you must live under for the rest of your life. You see hurdles as opportunities for growth into a new you, not as barriers meant to dissuade you from moving forward.

Having a fixed mindset means you believe that your skills, talents —basically, your lot in life—is fixed, and there is little you can do about it. If you believe you can't do something because you can't do it today, then you are following a fixed mindset.

If you examine yourself, you will notice there are areas in your life you have a growth mindset and areas where you are more fixed. If you have experience doing something, you will tend more on the growth mindset side. If you lack experience in an area, you will tend toward a fixed mindset.

You can have a growth mindset all the way, then hit a wall, and slide into a fixed mindset. What's important is to know that about yourself and then concentrate on fine-tuning your beliefs so you know, deep down inside, that if you put forth the effort, you will learn something, and you will get better at it.

A growth mindset is a critical asset for you to possess your whole life through.

A growth mindset also means that you're ready to hear somebody else's opinion, even if it's different from your own because you know you'll learn something new about them or the subject.

You've seen those people that live in a fixed mindset bubble. They get on social media, the internet, or TV/radio and spew closed-minded rhetoric for the world to hear.

You don't want to be that person. You want to be growth-oriented.

Yes, you want to have your own beliefs, morals, values, and the like, but you don't want to be so fixed in your ways that you can't even listen to someone else's opinion.

I live in Los Angeles, and there are a lot of extreme people here. The vegans, for instance, are a sector that can be very fixed in their mindset. They will argue, interrupt, and otherwise yell "no, no, no" anytime the conversation turns to carnivores versus herbivores—and trust me, they can turn any conversation toward that topic.

I say eat what you want to eat, believe what you want to believe, value what you want to value, but don't expect me to change my opinion because you raise your voice over mine.

I generally love my way of life, and I work on improving it daily because I know I can improve every day. I know I can grow into the person I desire to become. I have a growth mindset that allows me to change my opinion on things, to change my perspective, to change my perception, to change anything and everything I want to.

You have this too. You just have to exercise the mind-muscle so you can be in permanent growth mindset mode.

Open-minded: *adjective; willing*
to consider new ideas; unprejudiced

What Is a Growth Mindset?

A growth mindset is the capability to see everything as an opportunity to learn, grow, and experience life to its fullest. You can develop any talent, skill, or ability, no matter your background or current level of expertise.

A fixed mindset, on the other hand, believes that skills, talents, knowledge, and so on are relatively stationary and cannot be grown and cultivated.

A growth mindset realizes every single opportunity in life is a chance for growth. And then, if your mind is open to it, you will learn something, you will experience something you had not previously even considered. Even if you watch the same movie ten times in ten days, if you're wearing growth mindset goggles, I guarantee you'll see something new. You will understand something new about that movie each time.

A growth mindset in college (and in life) is imperative because you'll be introduced to countless situations that are unlike anything you've ever experienced before. Unless you went to a high school that had ten, twenty, thirty, or forty-thousand or more students, the likelihood that you've ever walked into a classroom where there are three hundred students is doubtful.

Whether you were raised in a metropolis or not, I doubt you had the level of diversity at your high school that you'll experience in college.

College is awesome! The social activities, organizations, clubs, groups, Greek life—everything so readily available to you and with little to no adult supervision. But if you go into it with a fixed mindset, cultivated through your parents, teachers, friends, preacher, town, city—literally everything you ever saw, heard, felt, or experienced—you will miss out on the wonderment that is college and the world.

Do you say or think things like the following statements?

"That's not what the cool kids did in high school."
"That's not what my parents would have wanted me to do back then."
"That's not what my parents would approve of me doing."
"That's not how I've always done it."

If so, you're going to miss out on fantastic opportunities to grow, to learn, to experience your life. This isn't somebody else's journey. You make the decisions now.

Even if your parents are paying your way and they've chosen your major, they're probably not deciding on your extracurricular activities. If they are that up your ass, you might need to have them talk to someone on campus so they ease up on you.

They're not deciding the topic for your term papers and assignments. They're not there to decide what you'll focus on within your major. They're not there to decide how you're going to feel, hear, see, or experience anything because you are deciding how you see everything through your eyes, how you experience them in your mind.

You choose how you're going to experience college and your life. Even if your parents are pushing you toward a particular major, there are still plenty of opportunities for you to make it your own. Walk into it with a growth mindset, and that major can be anything you want it to be.

A growth mindset is the ability to learn continuously and see the potential to arrive at an outcome from hundreds if not thousands of directions.

It's the ability to hear somebody else's side of the story and at least empathize with why they think that way. Humility is the art of overlooking dissimilarities in favor of the similarities and finding a connection.

A growth mindset is being able to meet somebody from a different nationality, with a foreign accent, a diverse background, a nontraditional upbringing, with divergent beliefs and values than you—and still get along with them. Better yet, you'll go beyond getting along with them—you'll like them, you'll want to get to know them better, and you'll make friends with them.

But if you only hung out with a certain kind of person in high school, then go to college and still only hang out with that same kind of person, you're not displaying much of a growth mindset. Instead of only dating a certain kind of person or only eating a particular type of food, develop a growth mindset: try something new, because in that uncomfortableness is the true essence of life.

A fixed mindset believes that you are only as smart as you were born to be.

You're only as talented as the skills you already possess.

You're only able to make friends with a certain kind of person.

Only this kind of person will like you because that's who's always liked you.

You're not pretty enough for that career.

You're not pretty enough for that person.

You're not smart enough for that job.

You're not this, that, or the other.

Any sentence that starts with I'm not, I can't, I don't, or I won't has its stem firmly planted in fixed dirt.

I am not, I repeat, I am not saying that if your friends aren't diverse, you aren't growth-oriented.

I'm not saying that if your partners are generally alike, you have a fixed mindset. And I'm not saying that if you don't want to do something, you are entrenched in a fixed mindset and are destined to live there forever.

First off, that's totally a fixed mindset way to see things, and it is also not for me to decide.

You know when you're giving it the "old college try" and when you are not. This is your life and your experiences. You choose how to live it. You decide how to see it.

You choose everything—that's the moniker of a growth mindset.

Do you want to be right or do you want to connect?
STEPHAN STAVRAKIS

A Growth Mindset Takes Practice

First, realize that your intelligence, abilities, skills, talents—everything about you—can grow and develop in whatever way you decide. Time and time again, I have read about how a scientist, inventor, computer science hobbyist, musician, or athlete pushed themselves through a perceived barrier and came out the other side with a new invention, a new record, a new personal best, a new or better something.

Nothing worth having in life has ever come easy, and nothing that ever changed the world was the first incarnation of the idea that presented itself. Even the original wheel was probably a rock—which was certainly not as streamlined as a wagon wheel or a wheelbarrow wheel. Everything can grow and evolve into a better version than the previous if seen through growth-minded eyes.

In writing this book, I fluidly moved through this experience with a growth mindset. I don't think my writing skills are the best in the world. I know my limitations, and I work on them. I'm not the fastest typist, for instance. I put effort into keeping my fingers in the correct position, practicing so I will get better.

I wrote the first draft to get the basics and the outline out of my head. After the first draft reached completion, I went back and chopped it all up. Now that you have my book in your hands, it looks and sounds very different from the first draft, and that's the point—that's where the awesome is!

> *The mental flexibility of the wise man permits him to keep an open mind and enables him to readjust himself whenever it becomes necessary for a change.*
> MALCOLM X

Action Steps Toward Having a Growth Mindset

1. Tell yourself you can figure this out. Literally, tell yourself you can do it, whether it's getting a good grade or making a new friend. Be decisive in the choices you make. Be action-oriented in the completion of doing it.

As you begin to complete things, learn things, and grow into this new you, you will increase your discipline and your abilities. It's a positive feedback loop. As you do things, you learn new things, and then you realize you can learn and do new things all the time. Creating that loop will become a self-fulfilling prophecy. You will know you can grow BECAUSE you are growing—which will fuel further growth.

2. Make a plan. A fixed mindset will either creep in or come in like an avalanche when you don't have a strategy. Reverse-engineer the project from completion to the blank piece of paper or computer document in front of you.

How do you envision it upon completion?

Now go backward and note each step along the way. That is your strategy . . . for now. It's going to change—that's the point of having a growth mindset. Build your strategy now knowing it will morph and evolve along the way.

3. Do not allow anyone else, let alone you, to tell you it's not possible. From the light bulb, to penicillin, to the internet, to online shopping, to social media, to the iPhone—all of them, and thousands of other inventions that changed our world, were once just visions by an inventor. Those visions only came to fruition because the inventors overcame the hurdles that inevitably arrived along their creative journey.

4. Replace the thought of "I'm failing" with the strength of "I'm learning." There is no failure, only feedback. You are not failing— you are learning better ways to do something.

5. Work your ideas to completion. The best way I have learned to show myself I can do anything is to do the things I say I'm going to do.

I want to lose weight and build muscle, so I eat healthfully and go to the gym.

I want to go on a speaking tour, so I put together my speech and contact schools.

I want to make new friends, so I go to the places people with similar interests as mine go.

Whatever example I could write here, you already have another fifty examples on the tip of your tongue. If you tell yourself you want to do something, then do it.

Be tenacious. Show up every day and do your best, and each day, your best will get better.

6. Stop seeking approval from others. Putting your energy into gaining others' approval is a fruitless endeavor because you will never attain 100 percent approval from everyone.

Do it for yourself. Do it because you have to look yourself in the mirror and be comfortable with the person looking back at you.

Tell yourself you can achieve whatever you set your mind to.

Don't let anyone tell you it's not possible.

Be disciplined and work your plan to completion.

Don't worry about other people's opinions of you and your goals, dreams, work, or accomplishments.

You are either growing in the sunshine of a growth mindset or dying in the shade of a fixed mindset.

You decide.

Every time.

That's a fact.

Google it.

What if . . .

Is what you are experiencing a fixed way of thinking or just a lack of prioritization? Knowing what you can and cannot prioritize is a massive part of positive habit creation, courage, and decisiveness. Not being able to prioritize something is not negative thinking.

It's not that you don't have enough time in your day to do all the things that you want; it's that you can only prioritize so many things in your day, week, month, year, or life.

What is it that you really, really, really want? (Hi, *Zoolander* reference.) Have the courage to make a decision, act upon it, have the discipline to work on it consistently, and be flexible as your plan plays out.

Have enough of a growth mindset to start. That's it—that's all you have to do.

And please remember, you can only prioritize so many things in your life.

Let's suppose somebody says, "Hey, we're going to do a river cleanup on Saturday; wanna come?" But you've already committed to a study group session. It's not that you can't go clean up the river; you could, but you're committed to the study group, so that's the priority. It's not that you don't have the time— you have the time, but you've already prioritized something else.

I talked about this with Thom Rigsby in episode two of the *College Success Habits* podcast. Priorities and focuses for your days, weeks, months, semesters, etc., are significant aspects in growing you toward your "meant to be."

It's all in your prioritization. You might prioritize something for a day, week, month, or semester, and later realize it is no longer serving you. That's OK. Now you know. There's no indecisiveness there. You made a decision, it started to play out, you realized it wasn't what you wanted it to be, so you move on.

Pivot—make a new a new decision and move on it. That's not quitting. It's re-prioritizing.

Having a growth mindset means you're open and willing

to try, do, and experience new things and grow through those experiences.

A fixed mindset says "I will never be good at the guitar." That's not true. If you were to start practicing, even thirty minutes a day or thirty minutes a week, and you did that consistently for a year, you would be better than if had you not done any of that.

Now, are you going to be on a stage selling out arenas? Maybe so; maybe not. You probably can't practice the guitar for thirty minutes a week and then in a year—in just a mere twenty-six hours—be able to start a band and be performing at arenas. That's not a fixed mindset; that's merely rational thinking.

But to say that you could NEVER play an arena is a fixed mindset because you haven't prioritized practicing the guitar. Practice the guitar five hours a day, every single day for a year. I bet you'll be band-ready.

If you're not great at writing essays, then write a paper about something you learned each week. It doesn't have to be a fifty-thousand-word thesis, but it certainly could be a one-pager about why you liked a particular book, article, or whatever.

Be decisive. Take action. Embrace discipline. Prioritize.

You're in college now, so step into the new you. Take your shot.

If you've ever wanted to have a particular hobby—do it.

If you've ever wanted to try a specific activity—do it.

Almost everything you've ever wanted to do or try is available on campus or within city limits.

The fixed mindset says "I don't know how to do that" or "I can't do that."

A growth mindset would say those same statements and end the sentence with "yet."

A fixed mindset says "I only draw stick figures, and that's all I know how to draw, and that's all I'll ever know how to draw." Then you never try to draw again or get any better.

I don't currently draw well. I'd like to draw better, but I don't prioritize it, so I'm not going to improve. It's not that I think I couldn't become a decent artist—I'm just not inspired to prioritize it. Not getting into drawing isn't a fixed mindset; it's me deciding there are other things I'd rather do—like write this book, give speeches, or host workshops.

A fixed mindset tells you that you only have a certain level of intelligence, talents, skills, and abilities. If you want a more growth-minded mentality, start putting yourself in situations where you have to grow, you have to learn, and then new experiences will become the default behavior, not the exception.

It doesn't matter how slow you go as long as you don't stop.
CONFUCIUS

Summary

- Having a growth mindset means: you are ready to learn new things whenever presented with them, you believe you can learn new things, and you know your current skills and talents are not the ceiling you must live under for the rest of your life.

- A growth mindset is the capability to see everything as an opportunity to learn, grow, and experience life to its fullest. You can develop any talent, skill, or ability, no matter your background or current level of expertise.

- A growth mindset means you're ready to hear somebody else's opinion, even if it's different from your own because you know you'll learn something new about them or the subject.

- A fixed mindset believes that skills, talents, and knowledge are relatively stationary and cannot be grown and cultivated.

Action steps to work through and follow. Write these down and go through them regularly.

1. Tell yourself you can figure this out.

2. Map out a plan.

3. Do not allow anyone else, let alone yourself, to tell you it's not possible.

4. Replace the thought of "I'm failing" with the strength of "I'm learning."

5. Work your ideas to completion.

6. Stop seeking approval from others.

Questions to ask yourself, work through, and follow. Write these down and go through them regularly.

Growth mindset with yourself:

- Am I viewing challenges as opportunities?

- Do I view setbacks as learning opportunities or failures?

- Am I rewarding my growth-minded actions?

- Am I taking ownership of my attitude?

- Am I seeking outside approval?

- What do I need to learn to get better at this task, assignment, or skill?

- Am I enjoying and valuing the journey or focused solely on the destination?

Growth mindset with others:

- Am I focusing more on being understood or understanding?

- Am I asking questions or waiting to respond?
- Am I listening intently to learn about the other person or am I thinking about what I'm going to say next?
- Am I asking questions or making statements?
- Do I feel the need to add to the conversation with "and" or "but"?
- Do I block others from talking?
- Am I embracing humility by overlooking the dissimilarities in favor of the similarities?

Important:

- Do I believe that the only thing that limits my ability is my mindset?
- Do I believe I can accomplish whatever I prioritize and focus on?
- Do I recognize when my fixed mindset is taking over, and do I have a plan in place for overcoming it?

Hint: This book is an excellent roadmap for establishing that plan.

DEVELOP A GROWTH MINDSET

Open-minded people embrace being wrong, are free of illusions, don't mind what people think of them, and question everything—even themselves.
AUTHOR UNKNOWN

Open-minded people don't care to be right; they care to understand. There's never a right or wrong answer. Everything is about understanding.
AUTHOR UNKNOWN

The mind is like a parachute; it only works when open.
AUTHOR UNKNOWN

Whether you think you can, or think you can't, you're right.
HENRY FORD

Challenges make life interesting— overcoming them makes life meaningful.
JOSHUA J. MARINE

CHAPTER 2

CULTIVATE COURAGE

Courage is the most important of all virtues because,
without courage, you can't practice any other virtue consistently.
MAYA ANGELOU

Courage: noun; the ability to do something that frightens you

Why Is Courage Important?

College courage is basically like "real world" courage, except you are more accountable in the "real world." In college, you can get a pass based on immaturity, naivety, or a "kids will be kids" mentality.

To me, courage is the ability to take risks, not settle for less, and realize that this is a fantastic opportunity to completely revamp, renew, rejuvenate, and rebirth a more evolved version of yourself.

College is your chance to build the strongest foundation possible. I don't want you saying you weren't informed. I don't want you regretting missed opportunities when you hit thirty or forty—which will happen crazy quick.

When I look back at how I entered college, I was courageous because I moved away from home and went. I was courageous because I left everything I had grown accustomed to, radically altering my life—but I also entered into that stage of my life with a fair amount of self-imposed limitations regarding who I was and what I was going to be able to achieve.

I was so young, so immature, so low on the emotional maturity scale that I was very ill-prepared for the college journey. I am amazed I survived those first few years.

There was a lot of fear in my life back then. I went to Ball State University with a lot of emotional baggage, a ton of fear and anxiety, and little actualized courage.

I wasn't generally popular in either of my high schools. My family moved frequently, and even when we finally stayed somewhere, my personality tended toward being very energetic and outgoing. Some classmates liked that about me. Others did not.

Then came the crushing blow when my parents announced their divorce weeks before I was to graduate high school. My mom and sister moved to Florida on my eighteenth birthday, and that same night, I got stoned for the first time at a Pink Floyd concert. Three weeks later, I took acid at my first Grateful Dead show.

After that Dead run, I met my new college roommate at a Wendy's in Franklin, Indiana, where he told me he had a supreme connection to LSD and could keep our minds tripping out for our whole college career.

So yeah, that happened.

When I arrived at BSU, I wanted to make lots of friends quickly. I wanted to go to parties. I wanted to meet women. I wanted to have fun, fun, fun. I didn't know much about the Greek system outside of the movie *Animal House*, but I learned quickly enough.

I had barely settled into college before I joined Sigma Phi Epsilon. I didn't give a moment's thought into the process of figuring out who I was, what I wanted, or where this adventure was going to take me. I was naive as hell, eyes half-open, with a beer in one hand, a joint in the other—and my fraternity was against all of it. Opposed to the top of the mountain, they were.

I jumped into the partying/addiction crowd without a second thought . . . well, there was some thought. I remember telling myself, in the entryway of my dorm, Painter Hall, that if I lit this cigarette on my way to class, I would henceforth become addicted to nicotine and one day I'd have to quit. I lit the cig, smoked it all up, and that was about the end of my self-awareness with myself and the partying choices I was making.

I made a ton of friends because the most accessible social circle to join is the partying/addiction one. I attended all the huge parties people talked about the next day. I felt popular. I felt accepted. I felt happy at night and hungover in the morning.

I thought I was courageous because I was leaping away from the old Jesse and becoming a whole new version of myself. I actually believed my adultness was affirmed based on my ability to party my ass off and not die in the process.

Sigh . . . I had no idea what courage was, is, or would be.

I was afraid of sitting in the dorm, on a Friday night, and studying as I did in high school. I was fearful of not having anything to do over the weekend.

I was fearful in so many ways, and I tell you all of this so you are aware of how easy it is to slide into the intoxicated social circle instead of being yourself and making real, meaningful friendships.

Drinking buddies and buddettes have a low propensity rate of turning into lifelong besties.

You should have the courage to be yourself. You should have the courage to do what you want to do when you want to do it. Often that's going to mean staying in and taking care of your actual college responsibilities and not going to the next "biggest party of the year," or whatever your friends say to entice you.

If courage is doing things that frighten you, strength in the face of fear or grief, the ability to act on one's beliefs in the face of danger or disapproval—then I was not courageous at all.

I was a drunk, and I was hiding from others and myself behind a veneer of liquor, weed, and acid. I was so scared of feeling anything meaningful that I chose to feel nothing.

While many of my frat brothers were off studying, earning good grades, involved on campus—you know, actually experiencing college—the rest of us would be sitting on the brick wall in front of the house, drinking our beers, our screwdrivers, just getting wasted.

I'll ask it again—why is courage important?

Because if you lack IT, then you also will lack self-awareness, self-confidence, self-esteem, self-worth, and so much more.

You will lack the ability to say no when yes is just so easy.

Giving in to social pressures isn't courageous; it's lazy. If everyone else jumps off a bridge to their deaths, joining them isn't facing your fear—it's dumb as hell.

And I haven't even touched upon the relationship of perfectionism and procrastination within courage and fear.

It takes courage to grow up and become who you really are.

E.E. CUMMINGS

What Is Courage?

So far, we've covered falling in with the wrong crowd as being a massive indicator of living a non-courageous, fear-based life.

Everyone is afraid of something; that is a fact. It's how you face that fear, manage that fear, deal with that fear, and begin to overcome that fear—which will speak volumes about your courageousness and character.

You want to transition into college with the most mindfulness and self-awareness as possible. Reading this book and listening to the College Success Habits podcast will get you way further ahead than binging on Netflix, playing video games all day, and getting drunk ever will.

This fear of being yourself—I have some theories about why this comes out so harshly in high school and college. We are very emotionally and socially vulnerable during those eight to ten years of our lives. I believe there's no other stage in our lives where we're more susceptible to outside pressures, bullying, chastising, and anything else you're experiencing (or have experienced).

Our fears have many root causes—so many that listing them would fill a book by themselves.

A few examples:

- How we were brought up
- How others treated us
- How we treated ourselves
- What we watched on TV and saw on the internet

Everything you've ever experienced became a part of your personality through your unconscious mind's ability to record everything, literally **EVERYTHING**, that's **EVER** happened to you.

Our brains are just like a computer. We have the desktop (our conscious mind), and we have the hard drive (our unconscious mind). The operating system is the combination of the two and is how we present ourselves to the world.

How do you define fear?

What do you fear the most?

What fears are holding you back from being the best version of yourself today?

I've read that public speaking is one of the most feared activities people can experience. I don't think it's the act of public speaking that people are afraid of. I think speakers are fearful of the judging eyes they think are looking back at them as they are presenting their speech.

Because of this, many people miss out on opportunities where they would be the center of attention because they cannot get over the fear of looking, sounding, or being whatever it is their mind has conjured up.

Courage is stepping into that fear and telling yourself that everyone else is just as afraid of what you are doing as you are.

The fact you are doing it gives you courage, gives you strength, and the bottom line is that most people in the audience want you to do well and are rooting for you.

Courage is managing and overcoming what it is you fear.

Step into the experience. Know that no matter how you perform, you will be better the next time because you've gone through the process.

Looking foolish lasts a moment; seen through social media, maybe it lasts twenty-four hours, seventy-two max—and then people will be on to the next social faux pas. The best thing about our society's short attention span is that no one will care what you did in a week, probably not even in a couple of days. Want proof? What happened in the news two days ago?

But you might regret what you didn't do for a long time to come, perhaps the rest of your life, and that is way worse than people pointing and laughing for a fraction of that time.

Here is a fact: The older you get, the more you will realize that no one was paying that much attention to you in the first place. We spend an excessive amount of time worrying about what others think of us. Then we get older and realize that everyone else was in their head, too worried about what others thought about them to be paying much attention to what we were doing.

CULTIVATE COURAGE

*Courage is the art of being the only one
who knows you're scared to death.*
EARL WILSON

How to Overcome Perfectionism and Procrastination

Remember when I mentioned perfectionism and procrastination?

Yeah, here comes some heavy-hitting reality here.

If you call yourself a perfectionist or if you procrastinate as default behavior, you are living in a state of fear.

You must seek to splinter yourself away from perfectionism and procrastination behaviors.

I have whole speeches and presentations about the first two descendants of fear being perfectionism and procrastination.

Think back to the cavemen. Hiding and running away from saber-tooth cats or looking for tasty berries to eat were high on our ancestors' daily to-do lists. Procrastination and perfectionism were foreign behaviors to a cave person determining if a berry would poison them, or if that big cat was around a boulder looking to make them its dinner.

Heading into the 2020s, Western society is a more civilized world, one where we're able to substantially reduce or eliminate many random acts of violence and death—well, for the most part. So the courage you need is quite different than that of our ancient ancestors. However, our brain hasn't been evolving as fast as our society and culture has. Our mind is still living with the idea that if you feel fear, then it's a life-or-death situation.

But those aren't the situations we're finding ourselves in 99.9 percent of the time.

If you want to risk your life, feel free to get wasted and walk through a dark, lonely park at 3:00 a.m. You can get that feeling walking through Hollywood or Skid Row around the same time too.

You can find yourself in some scary situations if you try, but that's not where you want to be, so I'm going to assume you are wise beyond your years and stick with plausible situations from here on out.

OK, back to perfectionism and procrastination.

If you're finding perfectionism and procrastination as part of your daily habits, you should start a conversation with yourself about that immediately.

When people say, "I am a perfectionist," I want to call bullsh*t on them right away. You think you are a perfectionist because you tinker with something to exhaustion or because you meticulously reread a paper seventeen times before you turn it in? Is that being perfect, or is it just passing something over in your mind enough times that you think you have finally done it to your level of perfection?

You will not achieve perfect, in everyone's eyes, ever. Even you will be able to find a flaw in something you once thought perfect if you step back from it long enough. I'm pretty sure I will locate an error in this book once it's published. I have found typos in some of the best books I've read. Even the best proofreader or copyeditor lets the occasional misplaced apostrophe, period, or synonym slip through

A "perfect ten" in gymnastics doesn't even exist anymore, but back when it did, no doubt someone, somewhere, saw imperfection in Mary Lou Retton's vault in the '84 Olympics.

Perfectionism stems from a fear that one's work will be judged as being less than perfect.

The desire to be perfect could keep you home from a meeting or keep you from volunteering for the project lead because you think you can't possibly be the best person for the position or have a great idea that people will follow.

My fear of being seen as imperfect ruled my life for years. My fear of being judged, my fear of failure, my fear of being comfortable in my own skin overruled my rational mind for two decades and kept me in a revolving door of drunk-hungover-recovering-regretting-drunk for half of my life.

It's the same with procrastination.

I have procrastinated because I didn't know how to do something.

I have procrastinated because I was afraid I wouldn't be great at something new.

I have procrastinated because of not knowing what would happen once I made a choice and moved on it.

This book could have been like that. I could have easily procrastinated for months, or even years, because of the fear that it wouldn't be perfect. Then five years from now I'd be going around telling people I am working on this book—but still, no actual book for people to read would have materialized.

George R.R. Martin can say whatever he wants about why he hasn't finished the last two books in his *Fire and Ice* series but, to me, the bottom line is that he's afraid of the cultural backlash if they suck.

Now that the whole world knows who Cersei, John Snow, and the Mother of Dragons are, and it's very possible people will be just as unhappy with the way he finishes their story as they were with HBO's version; I think he is procrastinating out of a perfectionist's mentality that serves neither him nor the reader.

You can sit on an idea for your term paper until the last week of the semester. Have fun with that. Your procrastination will lead to a less than perfect outcome even if you get an A.

Creating a positive feedback loop for either perfectionism or procrastination is not healthy for your stress levels going forward, nor will it result in your best work.

A positive feedback loop for perfectionism could be fussing over a term paper, getting an A, and thinking all that tinkering is what earned you the A—maybe so, maybe not (shrug.)

A positive feedback loop for procrastination could be putting off your part in a group project so another member does your work, and you figure people will always save your ass if you slack off—again, maybe so, maybe not (shrug.)

"But I'll have a job in the future that'll expect me to do a term paper's worth of work in three days!"

Really? That is your excuse for waiting until the last minute to start something? I've had those jobs. They want it done that fast because they understand momentum, perfectionism, and procrastination.

If they give you a month, you will take a month.

If they give you three days, you will take three days.

If they give you three hours, you will take three hours.

You have no idea what amount of revision time you will have in the future, so go ahead and provide yourself with as much as possible in college.

Once you know how to schedule out a term paper, learn to hit your markers throughout the semester, research, study, write, rewrite, edit, re-edit, and then turn it in on time and to the best of your abilities, you will forever have that skill set in your repertoire.

That is a valuable asset to have in yourself and one that's much harder to earn than the "cram it all into three days" skill set most of the student body adopts.

Success is not final; failure is not fatal;
it is the courage to continue that counts.
Winston Churchill

Action Steps: How Do You Develop Courage in Your Life?

Note: My seven powerful principles will serve you here. As we progress through the next five principles, look for ideas and inspiration to push through perfectionism and procrastination and develop courage.

1. Step through the fear of social awkwardness. No one is paying much attention to what you are doing, and if, by chance, someone is, they are too busy ridiculing you to get anything of note done in their life. Let them be shallow and without integrity while you gain the experience. Win-win for you.

2. Be grounded in the idea that not everyone will like you, but many will. Be who you want to be. Be around the people you want to be around. Don't hang with the people who want you around because you act like they want you to act.

3. Ask yourself why you feel fear in this situation.

- Why do I feel this fear?
- What is this fear's origin point within me?
- How can I overcome this particular fear?

4. Step into the fear and do it anyway. You cannot eliminate all fear; sometimes you'll have to do something even though you're afraid. In my experience, just going through whatever is making you afraid will relieve most of the fear and doubt. You know you have done this in other areas of your life. Go back to a time when you overcame a fear. What were you doing? How did you overcome it? I will bet you anything the "how" was as simple as deciding to take action and doing it.

What If...

What if fear overwrites your courage?

Step back from what it is you're afraid of doing and ask yourself what you are actually fearing.

Is it fear of being judged?

Is it public and social ridicule?

Are you behaving less than the best version of yourself?

Being more than? (A fear of standing out for good grades and/or accomplishments is a real thing.)

There are endless questions and infinite answers. The key here is realizing the worst thing that can happen is a feeling, and feelings change, become less uncomfortable, and just plain go away over time.

Walking through your fears, experiencing the emotions, and moving through the feelings are essential skills most people don't even think to put on their resumés.

What if you're still having issues with courage?

Sometimes you have to do it afraid.

Fear is a reaction. Courage is a decision.
Winston Churchill

Summary

- Courage is the ability to take risks, of not settling for less, of realizing college is a fantastic opportunity to completely revamp, renew, rejuvenate, and rebirth a more evolved version of yourself.

- Be aware of how easy it is to slide into the intoxicated social circle instead of being yourself and making real, meaningful friendships.

- Everyone is afraid of something; this is a fact. It's how one faces that fear, manages that fear, deals with that fear, and begins to overcome that fear that speaks volumes about their courageousness and their character.

- The older you get, the more you will realize no one was paying that much attention to you in the first place. We spend an excessive amount of time worrying about what others think of us. Then we get older and realize everyone else was in their head, too worried about what others thought about them, to be paying much attention to what we were doing.

- You must seek to splinter yourself away from perfectionism and procrastination behaviors.

Action steps to work through and follow. Write these down and go through them regularly.

- Step through the fear of social awkwardness.
- Be grounded in the idea that not everyone will like you, but many will.
- Ask yourself why you feel fear in this situation.
- Step into the fear and do it anyway.

Sometimes you have to do it afraid.

Questions to ask yourself, work through, and follow. Write these down and go through them regularly.

- How do I define fear?
- What do I fear the most?
- Why do I feel this fear?
- What fears are holding me back from being the best version of myself today?
- What is this fear's origin point within me?

- How can I overcome this particular fear?
- What will my life be like when I overcome this fear?

Important

- Is this fear coming from perfectionism?
- Is this fear sparking procrastination?
- Is this fear coming from what I think others will think or judge about me?
- Is this fear coming from my own self-judgment?

I learned that courage was not the absence of fear,
but the triumph over it.
NELSON MANDELA

CHAPTER 3

BE DECISIVE

Decisive: adjective; 1) the ability to make decisions quickly and effectively; 2) the conclusive nature of an issue that has been settled or a result that has been produced.

Why Is Decisiveness So Essential?

When I started looking for jobs after college, it was a bleak picture. I was interviewing for gigs I found on Craigslist, and I was not happy with the prospects. The jobs I wanted—working at journalism-oriented establishments and anything related to that field—were not clamoring for my services.

Perhaps it was because I wasn't really in the mood for those jobs, or maybe it was my lazy interviewing techniques. Either way, it seemed that only sales jobs, restaurants, and banks were saying yes, and the thought of clocking in day after day for those companies didn't appeal to me.

See, I took journalism as my major because I wanted to live an adventurous life filled with exotic travel, exotic food, exotic women, exotic, exotic, and more exotic. That's all I wanted from my first job out of college. I know, that's ALL?

I did not spend twelve years in college to graduate and find myself behind a bar or a banker's desk refinancing home loans. So when I found a gig overseas working for a media company that put together investment reports, I jumped at the chance. It was journalism-oriented and travel-heavy—as in passport-necessary.

I went all-in on the interview and knocked it out of the park. I was hired on the spot and told I'd be leaving for Belgium in less than two months.

It was a no-brainer to take that job. The company didn't seem as legit as I'd hoped, but the allure of traveling and adventure spoke way too loudly for me to go in any other direction.

I was decisive to the point that I overlooked some red flags and charged forward headfirst.

The experience was amazing. In nine months, I lived in, traveled to, and visited fifteen countries. I hugged the Petronas Towers and almost got stuck in Cuba. I lived next door to a brothel in Singapore and on the beaches of Nassau.

I chose decisively to take that gig because it was pretty much everything I wanted in a first job. When it was time to leave that company (the red flags were much more prominent and brighter nine months in), I chose just as decisively to move back to the states.

Decisiveness won't always appear as such a natural choice. There will be times—many, many times over—when the path you should take will not be so clear.

Being decisive in that interview and taking that job was the best decision I could've made for myself. My decisiveness opened up a whole new world to me, one that I was desperate to experience.

That's why decisiveness is essential. Without it, we miss out on life-changing opportunities.

Be decisive. Right or wrong, make a decision. The road of life is paved with flat squirrels who couldn't make a decision.
AUTHOR UNKNOWN

What Is Decisiveness?

Decisiveness is the ability to make a clear choice when presented with many options. It's also the practice of moving forward on your decision with confidence and then learning from the experience.

Making a decision and then questioning yourself every step of the way is not decisiveness.

Math or English at 8:00 a.m.? Choose and move on. University of _____ or _____ State University—choose and move forward. This major or that major—choose already!

Of course, you want to take some time to make the huge decisions, but I generally believe you know deep down in your heart what you want to do. That being said, how you decide to be decisive is almost as important as the act of being decisive.

Flippantly throwing a dart might seem like the best way to choose when you are in the throes of a self-induced stress avalanche. However, in the long run, leaving your life up to the skill of throwing a dart straight is a horrible way to make life decisions. Chance is no way to pick a university or major.

Our inability to decide can lock us up for prolonged periods and give us the illusion that we are doing something by "taking our time" to make a choice.

Do not allow indecision to clog your mind and get in the way of action, which we'll cover in the next chapter. Think about all the tiny decisions you need to make every day.

When you walk into a restaurant and can sit anywhere you like, how easy is it for you to choose a table?

When you look at the menu, and all the options are available to you, how easy is it for you to choose an entree (cost aside)?

When you open up your closet in the morning, how easy is it for you to choose an outfit? Shoes? Which backpack or purse you'll use that day?

Life is filled with little decisions. If you get caught up with indecisiveness over these tiny ones, how are you going to handle the huge decisions: your major, your living situation, your job? What if you can only pay one of these bills: cell phone, electric, or internet? Which one wins?

Start thinking about how you manage the small decisions versus the big ones. It might seem insignificant which fancy latte you want from Starbucks, but when that indecisiveness starts creeping into other areas of your life, you will need to have a firm decision-making protocol habit in place.

Decisiveness is a characteristic of high-performing men and women.
Almost any decision is better than no decision at all.
BRIAN TRACY

How to Be Decisive

The essence of being decisive is easy! Just make a decision and run with it. Go! Move! Onward Hooooe!

Make a choice and let it play out. Give it 100 percent effort all the way through. Do not stop a month in because it feels uncomfortable or scary.

Discomfort is a signal that you are growing, learning something new, and most likely is the result of you genuinely becoming the person college will influence you to become.

Choosing a major is life-altering, and one you should be thoughtful in determining, but overthinking it and taking the summer to select it is just buffering yourself from the action of deciding.

I'd be willing to bet that if you were asked to decide on what school to attend, what major to choose, or which class to take at 8:00 a.m., the chances are pretty good you'd know right off the top of your head which path you wanted to take. Any hesitation stems from listening to other opinions and influences instead of your own.

Did you choose your major because it was forced upon you by your mom, dad, preacher, teacher, or some dude on TV telling you how to do you?

If so, that's no bueno.

Following someone else's path for your life is how you find yourself working crazy hours at a job you hate. You might work crazy hours, or you might hate your job, but existing in both places at once leads to a myriad of emotions, and most are not favorable.

I've heard TED Talks on following your passion and choosing a career that way. Other TED Talks have said the opposite because your passions change as you age.

When I was a kid, I was very passionate about sports cards, transformers, and video games. How can passion toward sports collectibles, robots, and Mario Brothers become a career? I could be in robotics. I could develop video games. I could own a sports card store. You can take any passion from your childhood and turn it into your future job.

Ross Geller, from *Friends*, always loved dinosaurs when he was a kid. As an adult, he was a geologist at a New York City museum. Sure, it's just a TV show, but people who work with dolphins probably loved them when they were kids.

You can actually choose something you've always really enjoyed as your major, and there is always a way to turn that into a well-paying job.

My mother used to tell me, "If you are the best at something you can make a million dollars no matter what job it is." Think about that. If you're the best at something, you could make a million dollars. Just own the business.

Sure, it might take you twenty years to make that million, but you can do it if that's your focus. I might have to open twenty baseball card shops to make seven figures a year, but Mom's mindset is on point.

No matter what it is, you can turn it into a viable career option. Just don't be so indecisive that you wind up spending your freshman and sophomore years going back and forth instead of choosing and experiencing.

Changing your major eight times, continually dropping and adding classes, switching professors, wanting to move from one dorm to the next, switching jobs—that's some pretty energy-draining stuff to be putting yourself through. At some point, you'll end up second-guessing yourself anyway, so just choose one way or another.

You can be successful no matter what you choose, and your perception of success determines what that looks like for you. It is not for others to decide for you. You are living your life, not theirs.

So here are my action steps to becoming the Jedi of Decisiveness.

1. *Consider everything.* Self-imposed limitations are one of the biggest banes to human existence. "I can't," "I don't know how," "I never have; therefore, I won't" are not sentences you will believe about yourself any longer.

Give yourself all of the options.

Every.

Single.

One.

You are in college—this is the best time of your life to experiment with your potential.

University life IS the time to make mistakes— which aren't really mistakes but choices you made that didn't turn out how you'd have liked.

You are starting fresh. Start making brand-new decisions. High school is in the rearview mirror. Who you were then is not who you have to be in college. In fact, you must evolve. It is your duty as a co-ed, let alone a human.

You are on the journey of a lifetime. Once you are out of school, you will most likely not have this environment of growth at your disposal.

College isn't the end of your evolution, trust me. I have lived many lives since my cap and gown day, but not since then have I found an overall environment where everyone around me was pushing themselves toward achievement and great things.

Compared to major cities, college is way more condensed, people are generally within about six to eight years in age to one another, and there is a general naivety on campus you won't come across again on that scope.

2. Now consider a lot less. I call it the paradox of choice. It's when you have so many things to choose from that you can't pick between any of them.

I saw this frequently when I worked at restaurants and bars. Tell people they can sit wherever they want, and they'll go back and forth or stand there debating with each other. The menu is another problem area. Have you ever been to a Cheesecake Factory? They have a fifteen-page menu! How in the heck does anyone choose an entree?

To me, the key is crossing off as many things on your list, based on whatever criteria works for you. Beef, chicken, or seafood? Now that gigantic menu is whittled down to less than ten dishes. Booth, bar, or table? A lot fewer choices when you've figured that out.

You can move into the land of indecisiveness and stay forever if you like—you'll just miss out on awesome experiences. Procrastination and perfectionism will haunt you till the day is long if you don't get it together and make a decision. When you feel them creeping up on you, that's your moment to step into courage.

Whether it's your daily to-do list, class schedule, or the meal you're going to prepare, become habituated to weeding out the options you know you aren't feeling connected to. Get them off your list ASAP.

The more you practice this, the quicker you'll be able to get a list of five to ten items down to two to three, and that's a more manageable number of choices.

3. Imagine you can't fail. "But Jesse, it's not that easy! If I could make a choice, I would have already made it."

I get it, I do. I battle with indecisiveness too, and I defeat it by asking myself these two questions:

"What if no matter how I chose, it was an absolute success?"

"What if I couldn't fail?"

The booth has the perfect air temperature, or the chicken is juicy and delicious.

Let's amp these examples up a notch.

I'm talking about straight As.

You love all your classes.

The campus is beautiful no matter the season.

All your professors love you.

Everyone who meets you is instantly attracted to your energy, enthusiasm, and love for life. You are the star of this world, and you're loving every minute of it.

Now, which decision are you most wanting to turn out that way? Which outcome are you drawn to the most? Slow down, take a breath, slow your train of thought, and ask your unconscious mind, "What do you really want to do?" Listen for the answer.

The first thing you think is generally the answer. Doubting

the first thought is letting the conscious mind's self-imposed limitations take over.

Don't be silly here and balk at this strategy if your first thought was to smoke pot, watch Netflix, and eat ice cream all day. You might want to ask the question differently or try to find a major that has that as the outcome of your time in college. I think Seth Rogen has that job actually.

4. Realize you can't fail because there is no failure, only feedback. And you can't get that feedback if you don't make a damn choice.

Failure is all in your perception of the outcome. It's always a perception issue. You choose how you experience the journey and how you look back at it.

If you don't make a choice, you won't get results. Check that: the act of not choosing is a choice in itself—it's just a crap-ass choice, a procrastination move meant to buy you more time to make a decision your inner self has already made, but you're unwilling to accept out of fear that you'll regret it later.

Reread that last paragraph a couple of times so it sinks in.

Just decide! Chicken or beef? Decide! If the dish sucks, there's another meal coming; you eat a couple of times a day at least.

Ball State University or the University of Florida? It took me seven years, but eventually, I tried both.

At UF, a friend once asked me if I regretted taking twelve years to graduate college. My response was simple and clear.

I said, "Why would I be regretful? I love my friends. I love my school—we just won a National Championship—and I enjoy the life I have created for myself."

Sure, I have wondered what life would have been like if I had tried harder at Ball State. If I hadn't turned to drugs and alcohol to bury my emotions, make friends, and be "cool."

Those choices led my friend to ask that question, and they've led me to this keyboard, typing this book for you to read, right now, on this day.

I don't see my twenty-plus years of addiction as a failure on my part. Hell, no! I got a ton of feedback on how **not** to live my life, and I take those experiences to heart every day—not just today, but all the future days to come.

Try this on for size. Say, "No matter what decision I make, it is not permanent. I can always choose something different once I have gained experience in this choice and have more information to consider."

If you paralyze yourself with fear, live indecisively, and choose nothing, you will have nothing new to consider when the choice is thrust in your face again, and this time you won't be able to buffer away from the decision-making process.

Feedback only exists when you have gained experiences. If failure does exist, and I still say it doesn't, it would come from not experiencing life to gain that feedback—and that itself is feedback.

5. Accept responsibility for your decisions. I have learned, the hard way, that every experience was a direct result of my actions and that I cannot place blame or rewards upon someone else without first taking 100 percent responsibility for the outcome. If I don't accept the results of my college experience, and my life in general, as the culmination of my actions, then I'm blatantly behaving immaturely and irresponsibly.

Have you ever listened to someone's advice, and when it goes to hell, they respond with, "You're the one who listened to me; you didn't have to"?

I don't get to release the responsibility of my choices to others, and neither do you. You are the one who has to live with the life you've created for yourself. No one else will live it for you.

Make your choice.

Don't let your parents decide.

Don't let your guidance counselor or academic adviser decide.

Don't let your siblings decide.

Don't let your partner decide.

You decide.

Even if your parents are paying your way, pushing you to become a doctor because of family tradition, there is a way for you to take the reins and make the decision your own.

You will be the one waking up at whatever hour it is and heading to class, studying for those exams, going to that job, working for the (wo)man or being the (wo)man. Choose wisely. It's only your life's path we're talking about here.

What's your perspective?

Do you see life as infinite?

It is.

Do you see life as limited and fixed?

It's not.

However you see it, this is your path to create, to live with, and all responsibility for it rests on your shoulders.

Once you make a decision, the universe conspires to make it happen.
RALPH WALDO EMERSON

What If . . .

You're in college; try new things out. You want to be a vegan, be a vegan. Then be a pescatarian, then a vegetarian—hell, eat only raw meat, under a pale moonlight, in the woods, if you want.

You can make those decisions and move forward with them.

So you're going to be a vegan—great. Give yourself a certain amount of time to try it out. Maybe it's indefinite, or thirty days, or three days, or three minutes, whatever it might be—just do it.

Don't let others beat you down and say things like "You're always trying something then quitting or changing your mind."

Yeah! That's the point of life. Try new things, do new things, be a new person.

Shave your head, dye your hair pink, get a nose ring, paint your toenails the color of the rainbow—**be yourself and not the person others want you to be.**

Here's another example:

You're assigned a research paper, and you can pick any topic you want. Let's say it's an environmental science class. Pick three things about the environment you care about, then figure out which one of those you want to spend fifty hours researching and building a paper around.

If your choices are water reclamation in Southern California, honeybee survival, and the overuse of water in Mid-Valley, California, pick the one you think would have the most significant impact. Pick the one that's going to teach you some skills you'll be able to use on future assignments. Just make a decision and move from there.

I talked about this in episode seven of the *College Success Habits* podcast. There's a procrastination learning style where somebody who's indecisive goes back and forth, not making any decision.

My guest in episode six discussed this. It would be five hours after she gave the art assignment and one student is already four-and-a-half hours into designing it, while another student is still over there trying to figure out what it is they want to develop. They've missed four-and-a-half hours of productivity. They missed out on four-and-a-half hours of working on something and figuring out if they like it. They have zero feedback because they have taken zero action.

I could have been extremely indecisive about what I wanted each one of these chapters to read like and what I wanted to cover in this book. Ultimately it came down to just writing the damn thing.

Strategize, plan, write, edit, re-edit, then send it to the publisher.

I have no doubt, once this is in my hands—when I can feel it, see it, smell it (is that weird?)— I'm going to think of seventeen things to change or add.

Great! I'll write the second edition.

Don't allow indecisiveness to mute your talents, skills, and passions.

I chose telecommunications. Then I decided on journalism. Then I wanted photojournalism, then copyediting, then graphic design, then . . . I had like eight concentrations in my major, lol.

The fear of making a decision is a fear that it will be the wrong decision, that you'll regret it, that you'll wish you had chosen something else, but there is no mistake in making a decision. (Unless it's drinking and driving or hurting someone else—those are the wrong decisions every time.)

There is no failure, only feedback.

Make a decision.

Move on it.

When you get to the outcome, you'll either see it as positive or negative depending on **your** perspective, not someone else's.

Experience is priceless, so opt to see it as a positive outcome.

Now, make another decision.

If you're at a restaurant, staring at the menu for twenty minutes, trying to figure out an entrée, there's always another meal.

There's another day to try on a new outfit.

There's another day to try on a new pair of shoes.

There's always another day to go to a different event and meet different people.

Don't be so indecisive that you miss a new experience. Change is inevitable. You are not going to be the same person tomorrow as you are today or were yesterday. When you are halfway through the first class, halfway through the first semester, at the end of your freshman year—so much about you will be different.

You can choose a career path that you know will give you money. That's a very decisive decision.

You might realize something about your major sucks while you're still in school, or you might wake up fifteen years from now in middle management at Dunder Mifflin cursing your business degree. You might be making six figures a year, but you hate your lack of schedule flexibility, no vacation time, and not seeing your kids playing sports or in the school play.

You made a decision, and at that point in your life, if you decide you want to have more time, you want to have more flexibility - then you make a new decision there.

Just make a decision. Have I said that enough yet?

The way to develop decisiveness is to start right where you are, with the very next question you face.
NAPOLEON HILL

Summary

- Decisiveness is the ability to make a clear choice when presented with many options.

- It's also the practice of moving forward on your decision with confidence and learning from the experience.

- Making the decision, then questioning yourself every step of the way, is not decisiveness.

- Take time to make huge, life-altering decisions but

don't overindulge in that state—be aware of the role perfectionism and procrastination play in this indecision.

- Your inability to decide can lock you up for prolonged periods and give you the illusion that you are doing something by "taking your time" to make a choice.

- Life is filled with every day, little decisions you have to make. If you get caught up with indecisiveness over these tiny ones, how are you going to handle the huge ones?

Action steps to work through and follow. Write these down and go through them regularly.

- Consider everything.

- Now consider a lot less.

- Imagine you can't fail.

- Realize you can't fail because there is no failure, only feedback.

- Accept responsibility for your decisions and actions.

Questions to ask yourself, work through, and follow. Write these down and go through them regularly.

- What is the outcome I want to achieve?

- What is my why?

- What is my how?

- What is my hesitation?

- Am I trying to be perfect?

- Have I evaluated the best-case and worst-case scenarios?

- Have I eliminated the stress of making small decisions in my life?

Important:

- Am I fully aware of the roles perfectionism and procrastination are playing in my indecisiveness?
- Am I taking full responsibility for my decisions and actions?

Hesitation enlarges and magnifies the fear.
Take prompt action by being decisive.
DAVID J. SCHWARTZ

CHAPTER 4

TAKE ACTION

Action: *noun; the fact or process of doing something, typically to achieve an aim.*

Why Is Action Important?

Action is important because, without it, you might as well be a tree—just chilling there while life passes you. If you don't start anything, you never experience anything. Well, you experience something, it's just nothing of note.

Action is the essence of life. You arrived on this planet by taking action: "Hey, Mom, I'm coming out! I've had enough of this cramped womb—let's do this!" or something like that; I don't know—I wasn't there. Whatever you said, I am sure it was poetic.

You can't just sit on your couch and watch life through your smart TV, computer, or phone.

Once you've summoned the courage to make a decision, you have to act on it.

It took a mix of courage and decisiveness, and now you've chosen a thesis topic and a strategy for the project. Now it's time for action. Get in motion immediately. If you allow perfectionism or procrastination to start creeping in, you are succumbing to inaction.

Action is vital because it's the only way you'll know if the decision you made was the right one for you or not.

You are what you repeatedly do,
not what you repeatedly say you will do.
AUTHOR UNKNOWN

What Is Action?

It's simple. It's the act of doing something.

Once you've chosen your outfit, put it on.

Once you've chosen the dinner, order it.

Once you've chosen your shoes, wear them.

Once you've chosen to date someone, date them.

Action is insanely essential in college because you have everything at your disposal, a world of opportunities.

If you find someone intriguing, for whatever reason, dare to go up to them—in a non-psycho stalker kinda way, please. Don't procrastinate; walk straight up to them and be like "Hey, I haven't met you yet." Be decisive and introduce yourself. The worst-case scenario is you miss out on the best-case scenario—and that would super suck. Take your shot. If you miss, you miss, but you miss all of the shots you don't take (shout-out to Jordan).

I can assure you that the main regrets I have from my twenties and thirties, besides drinking them away, is the severe inaction in which I was firmly entrenched.

Once I got sober and examined my actions over the last two decades, I discovered that my inaction stemmed from procrastinating because of my desire to achieve perfection in everything I did.

Now I'm all about that action. I make things happen regardless of my level of expertise. I dare to step forward into stuff I've never done before. Doing otherwise would certainly short me from my best life and at the minimum leave me well below my full potential. I make decisions every single time they come up, and I act on them - because the only way to gain the knowledge I need to learn from all of these experiences is to step into action.

That's what action is to me.

It's doing something instead of buffering my decision-making in an attempt to feel productive because I am "thinking things over."

Words prove who you want to be; actions prove who you are.
AUTHOR UNKNOWN

How Do You Take Action?

Repetition is the key to remembering, so here it is again: agree to just do it! Do something, do anything, step forward, step in, raise your hand, volunteer, hire yourself—in other words, get moving!

Newton's first law of motion works well here. I know, I know—science.

An object at rest stays at rest, and an object in motion stays in motion, with the same speed, and in the same direction, unless acted upon by an unbalanced force.

Thus, the hardest part of getting started is moving from inertia—from standing still, sitting down, doing nothing—to taking that first step. Then it's up to you to figure out what that motion, speed, and direction will feel, sound, and look like.

"But Jesse, how do I get in motion if I'm frozen under inaction?"

Action steps in the action chapter—now that's some perfect synergy.

1.Get up and do something, anything, or maybe even the thing you actually need to do.

Start by cleaning your apartment.

Start by organizing a room.

Make your bed.

Put your clothes away.

Get your blood pumping.

Walk around your apartment complex.

Walk around your dorm.

Walk yourself to the kitchen and get the cleaners out.

Hightail it to the library and open the book already!

I love to get my body moving—push-ups, sit-ups, jumping-jacks, anything that gets my blood pumping and my energy level up.

Start, start, start doing something. You'll have time later, when you daydream, to ask yourself why you were so hesitant to start.

Now, don't let the above turn into a prolonged buffering session.

I like to clean, take walks, or work out because it's in those habituated actions I can let my brain go off and think about, brainstorm, or strategize the action steps I'll need to get the thing started and done.

The longer you wait to start something, the more fear, doubt, and indecision take over your thoughts. Have you ever seen someone and immediately felt compelled to introduce yourself? Have you then stood there, trying to think of the best icebreaker, only to say to yourself, "Never mind, they probably wouldn't like me anyway."

That's what happens when you don't just go.

2. Realize that the conditions to start will never be perfect. If you wait in your car for all the lights on your route to be green before you left you'd never put the car in drive. You will be waiting forever if you expect the conditions to be perfect.

You
will
always
be
waiting

I'm not a fan of definitives because rarely will something be always or never, but in this case, it's accurate every time.

Waiting is a future person's game, and there is only the here and now. The Chinese proverb "The best time to plant a tree was twenty years ago. The second-best time is now" couldn't be more accurate here.

Wait thirty minutes to start, and that's thirty minutes you'll be behind compared to the other version of yourself that jumped right in.

3. Stop paralysis by analysis in its tracks. Overanalyzing anything is an unfruitful endeavor. I could have overanalyzed this book from here to eternity. That would have been great for my analytical brain, which loves to think through every possible scenario, but not so great for getting this project off my desktop so I could start another project.

See, for me, I am all about action. I want to create everything my brain conjures up. I cannot just be chilling. Even on holidays and vacations, my mind is whipping up the next great thing I can do with my time.

If I paralyzed myself with the analysis, I wouldn't get anything started, let alone finished. My brain would be full of great ideas I never saw through to fruition.

So many people have the greatest idea, start it, then shelve it in favor of the next shiny object. I used to be one of these people. I would have multiple "great" projects going and rarely would any see completion.

This book is not one of those projects. I shelved everything else I was working on or wanted to work on until this arrived on my publisher's desk. I cannot have this book looming over everything else I want to accomplish this year.

Don't be the kind of person with great ideas who never sees them to the finish line.

My philosophy:

Get it done.

Learn from the experience.

Do it even better the next time.

That's my working philosophy with this book, the *College Success Habits* podcast, the *From Sobriety to Recovery* podcast, my website, my business card—everything I do runs through this philosophy.

4. *Take action every day.* That term paper that isn't due for three months—yeah, that's gonna be due before you know it.

Let's assume you've already implemented the last three principles. Now do something toward the completion of that term paper every single day. It could be jotting down a great idea on a piece of paper while out with friends. It could be recording a voice memo on your iPhone while driving. Once your brain knows you want something done, it will start feeding you suggestions on how to get there.

When you find yourself in **trance mode, any action so habituated as to take very little brainpower to perform**—that's where the yummy ideas spring out of the virtual clear blue. Driving your car, showering, brushing your teeth, getting dressed—the list goes on. Just start thinking about the term paper, and your brain will do its job. Those little brainstorms, juicy nuggets of ah-ha moments, will brighten your day when you go about actively working on the paper.

5. *Action sparks motivation.* Do you believe action creates motivation, or do you think motivation creates action?

I believe wholeheartedly that action creates the motivation that creates further action, and thus, initiates the positive feedback loop.

Are you waiting to feel motivated to clean that sink full of dishes?

Are you waiting to feel motivated to do laundry? Wash your car? Have an uncomfortable conversation with your roommate?

Wait long enough to do the dishes, and the ants, roaches, and mice will get you into action mode real quick.

That's not you feeling motivated; that's you chasing a rat from your house, and NOW you're in motion toward those dishes.

I can't recall ever feeling motivated to start a journalism story in college. Even as the deadline approached, it wasn't motivation that got me to start, but the stress of knowing an F would kill my GPA.

Have you ever said, "I get my best work done on a deadline crunch when the stress is eating me alive."

Really? Your *best* work? Have you tried it the other way? Where you plan it out, efficiently get it done, calmly walk into class, and turn in the assignment, knowing you had plenty of time to review and edit it.

We could debate this till our faces turn blue because inevitably there will be some of you who firmly believe your best comes out when the clock is ticking down.

You know what's even better than the last second, game-winning; shot, throw, catch, or goal? Not being behind in the first place.

6. *Breathe deeply and be present.* Get out of your head and into your body. Watch YouTube breathing exercises, get a meditation app, hell, just breathe deeply for four seconds, hold for four seconds, and exhale for four seconds. Repeat that till you're about to pass out and tell me if you aren't out of your head and in your body now.

Daydreaming about your strategy for completing a task is great for planning, but frequently being off in LaLa Land is counterproductive to getting the job done.

Get out of your head!

Even as I write this book, I have to yank myself back from drifting off because my mind loves to daydream of me playing guitar on the Santa Monica pier in front of raging fans—and I can't even play the guitar. Perhaps listening to Alt-Nation isn't the best background music. Next thing I know, the clock says a half hour has passed, and I'm still looking at the same line.

Breathe deep, stay in the present, and keep doing.

7. Distractions are inaction's best friend. We're nowhere near 1994. Back then, I only had to go to the library or favorite study zone, and as long as I didn't start talking to someone, I was in the clear to work, work, work.

Here come the 2020s, and the above scenario hasn't been the case for over a decade. Smartphones, the internet, social media, the bings, dings, chimes—you name it, and it'll distract you.

Back in the day, as long as I steered away from my friends and booze, I could stay motivated to keep at my task. Mind you, I didn't succeed at that often. Today countless things are vying for our attention. I'm amazed anything gets done.

Everyone has that friend with a plethora of ideas who doesn't get anything accomplished.

Don't have that friend? Might you be that friend then?

Don't be that friend. Put away the distractions. Set a time to start and a time to stop. Give your brain a victory, knowing it got that window of work completed.

There are few feelings better than setting a marker and hitting it—like this chapter. I gave myself a window to work on it today. From 1:30 to 3:30. Once 3:30 hits, I am done for the day. If I have more ideas pouring out or more things to say, I jot them down below this section and minimize the document. I told my brain it had this window, and it deserves its rest once 3:30 hits. If I feel compelled to continue, I can, but the time limit is really about not rushing to finish early.

I do this at the gym. My schedule allows for gym time Monday, Wednesday, and Friday from 1:00 to 3:00 p.m. I cannot leave early. I cannot blaze through the workout so I can leave at 2:00 p.m. That's not how this works. Keeping myself to that two-hour window ensures that I do all the exercises correctly, and with the right amount of rest between sets.

I am not allowed to play on my phone, answer texts, check email—nothing else but listen to music and workout. I generally finish my main workout in an hour and fifteen minutes, so then I get to use the foam roller to roll out my muscles. I do abs or glutes. I get to use the StairMaster or the rowing machine. I get to do anything in that gym, but I do not get to play on my phone, stare/flex in the mirror, or leave early.

Schedule a block of time for something and get it done in that allotted time. Try it on for size, and tell me you're not feeling super awesome when you leave the gym or library. Not rushing to finish reduces stress and keeps you focused on the activity.

I'm telling you—nothing feels better than the inner joy that comes from accomplishing a task to your fullest.

The only impossible journey is the one you never begin.
TONY ROBBINS

What If . . .

Be honest with yourself when it comes to downtime and self-care too.

Get up off your couch and start moving. If you think you're too exhausted and therefore you deserve to lie on your couch and watch Netflix all day instead of getting up and studying, ask yourself: "Have I been lying on the couch for three hours and my body's in chill mode or have I been running and running all day?"

If you're always moving, moving, moving, moving, and you sit down and find yourself falling immediately to sleep, then self-care and rest have been earned.

Decide to take a nap. Turn off your TV, phone, computer— whatever could keep your brain active. Fall asleep, and be OK with it because you're exhausted and you've earned this break.

But if you're not exhausted, you haven't gotten much done that day, and there are more priorities you need to accomplish, you must be able to push yourself so you can go to bed feeling like this day was a win.

Don't start looking for a way out of being productive. If you find yourself rationalizing your inactions, in your head or to others, it's a pretty good sign you are buffering away from action.

Go back to the beginning of this chapter and reread it if you find yourself rationalizing why it's cool that you binged another show for eight straight hours.

Thinking will never overcome fear, but action will.
W. CLEMENT STONE

Summary

- Action is the essence of life. You can't just sit on your couch and watch life through your smart TV, computer, or phone.

- Procrastination and perfectionism are hindrances to action.

- Action is vital because it's the only way you'll know if the decision you made was the right one for you or not.

- Action is essential in college because you have everything at your disposal, a world of opportunities.

- Make decisions every single time they come up, and act on them—because the only way to gain the knowledge you need to learn from all of these experiences is to step into action.

Action steps to work through and follow. Write these down and go through them regularly.

- Get up and do something, anything, or maybe even the thing you actually need to do.

- Realize the conditions to start will never be perfect.

- Stop paralysis by analysis in its tracks.

- Take action every day.

- Action sparks motivation.

- Breathe deep and be present.

- Distractions are inaction's best friend.

Questions to ask yourself, work through, and follow. Write these down and go through them regularly.

- What is the outcome I desire from this action?
- Am I expecting the conditions to be perfect?
- Where is over-analysis leading to procrastination?
- Am I worrying about what others will think?
- What would I do if I wasn't afraid of the outcome?
- Am I living a lifestyle that promotes physical, emotional, mental, and spirtual wellbeing?
- Is my social circle a positive influence?

Important:

- Am I true to my values?
- Am I living in integrity?
- Am I living with humility?
- Am I living with gratitude?

Trust is earned when actions meet words.
CHRIS BUTLER

Ideas without action are useless.
HELEN KELLER

CHAPTER 5

EMBRACE DISCIPLINE

Discipline: *noun; training that produces obedience or self-control, often in the form of rules and punishments if these are broken, or the obedience or self-control produced by this training; a particular area of study, especially a subject studied at a college or university.*

Why Is Discipline Important?

You have to have discipline in your life to accomplish what is truly important to you. I believe discipline is having self-control and determination over the distractions of life. It is pushing through perceived obstacles because I know I can figure anything out if I prioritize and focus on it.

Anything worth accomplishing is going to take many steps, stages, and a hell of a lot of time, and there are going to be hurdles; there is gonna be friction; there will undoubtedly be an imbalance you'll have to deal with at some point.

That's a fact.

Google it.

You will not achieve anything in life without having to overcome an obstacle you did not see coming. You can't prepare for everything.

Trust me. I've tried.

Do you have the discipline to get over the hurdles, barriers, and limiting beliefs you'll put in front of yourself?

Do you have the discipline to go to the gym three times a week?

Do you have the discipline to get up early to study before class?

Do you have the discipline not to go out drinking when you've got work to do?

Do you have the discipline to call your rents once a week because you said you would?

Do you have the discipline to be in a relationship?

Do you have the discipline to arrive to work on time and do the best job possible so you clock out knowing you've accomplished your best work?

Discipline is critical in life, not just in college—because it is through commitment to yourself that you experience everything life has to offer. And because of those experiences, you will discover what it is you like, want, desire, and love about yourself, others, and the endeavors you pursue.

Discipline brings freedom and peace of mind. If you know you are going to follow through on your commitments, you will be less stressed when you make them. You will gain peace of mind knowing you are a person who does what you say when you say it.

When you honor yourself by committing 100 percent, every time, no matter what, and don't give yourself an out, that is where you'll find the truth of discipline.

It's not what college teaches you; it's what you learn.
AUTHOR UNKNOWN

What Is Discipline?

Success in college, life, career, relationships, and importantly, personal growth and self-development, has two general components: intelligence and self-control. Self-control is a key element to success, and practicing it makes you stronger in your discipline moving forward.

When you make a decision, do you stick with it?

Do you push through the hard-knocks and difficulties?

When you honor your decisions, it becomes a healthy habit, which means it becomes something you start doing intuitively, without consciously or unconsciously thinking about a way out.

Lacking self-control shows itself in many ways. Perhaps you go out drinking and stay up late when you know you have to be up early for class. Your desire to "unwind" brings about a lapse in judgment, and you pay for it hard the next day. Your emotions and desires can bend and break your self-control if you are not mindful of the repercussions that will come from indulging in your whims.

The role of intelligence in discipline is not about your IQ. It's about learning your values, recognizing your limitations, and grounding yourself so you don't think you're the center of the universe.

We all have some impossible desires—like me quarterbacking for the Chicago Bears. Intelligent discipline pulls me back to the ground, where I can set more rational goals. These aren't self-limiting beliefs as much as they are "living in the real-world" goals.

Discipline can bring frustrations because it's through this stricter mindset that you realize you don't get to do whatever you want, whenever you want. By accepting limitations, you learn to face reality with self-assuredness, knowing that you can achieve almost anything if you prioritize and focus on it.

Look at it this way. You can't lose fifty pounds by sitting on your couch all day and eating six thousand calories. That's not a limiting belief; it's reality. Discipline allows you to realize this, and from there, you can strategize an actual way to lose fifty pounds.

Discipline is a beautiful thing. As you grow it in one area of your life, it naturally seeps into other areas.

When I got sober in 2017, my first act of self-discipline, besides not drinking anymore, was planning out a gym routine, starting it, and not stopping it . . . ever.

That physical fitness discipline got my daily schedule in order because I had to work out for two hours Monday, Wednesday, and Friday. By setting that window, the rest of my days began to form around that commitment to myself. Knowing every other day, I *had* to hit the gym helped me focus my time management priorities because there were other things I wanted to accomplish.

Of course, life happens while I'm busy making plans. Appointments and meetings pop up, clients and speaking gigs come calling, but otherwise the gym has held that two-hour time slot for three years and counting. I am flexible with the time slot when the need arises, so I am still hitting my three days a week goal.

That discipline led me to eat better, go to bed earlier, and schedule working hours for my projects—efficiently moving from one task to the next without letting the bings, dings, and chimes of my phone pull me away.

Discipline in one area leads to discipline in every area— guaranteed. You can take that to the bank.

I lacked discipline so much in my twenties and thirties that I'm surprised I'm alive. Seriously, I have some stories I tell from the stage you should check out when I come to your campus.

It turns out my best discipline was waiting for me in my forties.

Before that, I used alcohol, drugs, women, sports, video games, reading, and everything else to buffer me away from accomplishing things I claimed were important to me. So much for self-control, huh?

I thought I was "all about that action, boss," but I was so not. I thought I was accomplishing things, but I wasn't accomplishing anything meaningful because I didn't develop a well-thought-out strategy or plan, nor was I being disciplined enough to see it through.

You might've noticed the above paragraph sounding a lot like a limiting belief perspective and negative self-talk. I can see that, too, but I know I let countless opportunities slip by because of my indulgence in vices and distractions.

Sure, I graduated college, had amazing experiences, and made friends for life, but I stunted my development into adulthood due to my constant inebriation and otherwise blasé attitude toward my personal growth and development.

Now when I say I'll be at the gym Monday, Wednesday, Friday from 1:00 to 3:00 come hell or high water, I am there. I might move it around if I have to miss that day because of an appointment, but three days a week, for two hours, I am working out.

Now it is so routine that I do not have to talk myself into going. I do not have to bargain with myself; it is a habit, and it feels weird and abnormal when I have to miss it.

Do you have the discipline to turn your head away from the cookies and toward the Brussels sprouts?

Do you have the discipline to start a project that's not due until the end of the semester on the day it's assigned?

Discipline will be one of the most critical habits you instill in yourself in college, or high school, or middle school if you are blessed enough to be reading this with college so far off in the future.

I remember imposing video game limitations on myself in the summers of my elementary and middle school years. If I found myself playing them too much instead of being outside, I would pack the system up and put it in my closet.

One summer, after getting a couple Bs in math and science my seventh-grade-year, I grounded myself from playing Nintendo at my house. I had no choice but to play outside, read, or go over to Donovan's house and play Nintendo there.

See, my viewpoint on it was simple. If I played at my house, I would hole up in my room, shades lowered, and waste away the summer isolated from sunshine, knowledge, and friendships.

Side note: I got straight As my eighth-grade year.

> *Discipline is the bridge between goals and accomplishments.*
> JIM ROHN

How to Be Disciplined

The more you use your self-discipline, follow through, and honor your commitments, the more willpower and self-control you'll have for future use.

Discipline and willpower are two things you get more of when you use them. They are renewable resources, and you should actively use the hell out of them, so your mind and body generate a positive feedback loop around them.

When you honor your commitments, you begin to make that behavior a habit. When it's a habit, you effortlessly accomplish what you say you will. After a while, you won't even know what it's like to not follow through and do what you promised yourself or others you would do.

And once again, I have action steps. Ask yourself these questions, write them down, review them every day.

1. *What is your vision?* What is it you want your life to look like when you accomplish this task? What is it you want to experience from honoring this commitment?

Let's say you commit to losing weight.

What will your life look like when you lose this weight?

How will you see yourself?

How do you think others will see you?

What do you see your life being like when this weight is gone?

Can you run, jump, and play with others in a more carefree way?

Can you walk up the stairs without getting winded?

Can you finally skydive?

Picture yourself someplace you've longed to go with your improved body. Is it a beach, a mountain, a bar, a swimming pool, or sunbathing at the quad?

See your vision in your mind's eye and lock it in for future motivation when you're feeling blah and inaction-oriented.

2. *What is your "why?"* Why do you want to lose this weight? Why do you want to be in better shape? What is the driving force beneath this decision?

Knowing the why and picturing your outcome will help you stay disciplined and push you through those not so great days when you want to lie on the couch, binge on Netflix, and munch on Oreos.

Is your why so powerful that you jump off that couch, look in the mirror, and say, "Oh, hell no—get your ass to the gym!"

3. *Build a habit around it.* This is the formula for building a habit that will stick:

Cue → Craving → Response → Reward

It is also known as:

Cue → Response → Reward

Commit this to memory because this is how you build your habits—all your habits, both positive and negative, good and bad, powerful and weak. Habits can be utilized in place of discipline because a habit can be cued automatically and powered by the unconscious mind.

See a dessert you desire, but you've committed to being in better shape? Set a habit around the temptation to eat sugar. Your cue is seeing the sugary treat. The craving comes right behind it, so what will your response be?

You could drink a glass of water. You could drink six. You could aim to fill your belly full of non-caloric beverages. Then you won't feel like there's any room in your stomach for that tasty treat.

Whatever your response, it has to lead to a reward that will continue to motivate you to follow your new nutrition strategy.

Sidenote: Notice I didn't say diet.

The word *diet* has a negative connotation around it because it comes from a place of scarcity. Like, I want to eat this, but I am being an asshole to myself and depriving myself of this thing.

Don't be an asshole to yourself. Be awesome to yourself. Choose a nutrition plan that allows for some tastiness *and* is nutritionally sound a majority of the time.

The reward is imperative; it's perhaps the most critical part of this process because the reward solidifies the habit in place.

If you touch a hot burner on the stove and scorch your hand, you aren't going to make that a habit because the reward is third-degree burns.

If you skip the Oreo in favor of some water and carrots, the reward is being proud of yourself for sticking to your plan—for being decisive about your decision and not succumbing to instant gratification.

Another side note: If by chance you do opt for the Oreo, remember this sage advice—teeth don't taste.

When you chew the sweet treat all up and swallow it in under five seconds, you missed a ton of the enjoyment. Break the treat up with your teeth and then roll it around between the roof of your mouth and tongue. Spread it all over your palate so you can enjoy the sugary sweetness.

If you eat a whole Snickers bar in less than a few minutes, you're not eating it for the taste; you're eating it to fill an emotional void, and that action will lead you nowhere good.

My reward for not eating unhealthy items is the gratification I get knowing I won out over the scientifically tested, addictive treat.

Okay, this seems like the perfect time to touch upon FOMO and YOLO. I desire for you to be mindful of how you use those two acronyms to lead your decision making process and the significance they play in your general life. The "fear of missing out" and "you only live once" mentalities have the ability to yank you off course in the blink of an eye. These two mindsets will show themselves ferociously when vices are in play. Drinking on nights when you know you shouldn't. Binging on the hottest Netflix release. Eating things that you know will leave you feeling blah afterward.

I have tasted Cheetos. They are scrumptious. I already know this, but I don't eat them because they offer no nutritional value, and if I am going to hit my fitness goals, I can't be hanging out with Chester Cheetah on the daily.

The importance of setting a strong reward is the emphasis here. The habit of eating healthy won't stick long term if you feel the response to not eating the Oreo as depriving yourself of something you want. More on FOMO and YOLO later, as the importance of setting a strong reward is the emphasis here.

There is a lot of growth mindset work involved here. Getting in shape is a marathon event—meaning it's going to take you a long time to get to the proverbial finish line—while eating the Oreo is an instant gratification sprint. Sure, you feel something positive during the Oreo eating, but the aftermath is a total sugar buzz kill.

Gaining the Freshman-15 is a real thing in college. Hell, I've seen it balloon up to the Freshman-30 or 40.

Once you establish a positive feedback loop around your healthy eating habit, you can focus on strengthening it. With this loop, it will become easier and easier to walk away from Oreos in the future. This new habit of not eating sugary treats in favor of healthy fare will override the mind's discipline—meaning, you won't have to use willpower because you just won't want to eat the Oreo.

Picture it like this.

I used to drink booze like others drink water. When I quit, I turned not drinking into a positive feedback loop. Not drinking alcohol means that I am in control of my actions. It means that I am the best version of myself every day. It means that I made a decision, and I am sticking with it even when life and stress come at me from all directions.

I can be around booze all day long now, and there is no desire to consume it. Yes, a craving comes here and there, and it also leaves pretty quickly. The key, for me, is to realize the outcome of me drinking isn't just what happens right then but the aftermath of what will come the next morning and every moment after that.

Side note: binge drinking is something almost every college co-ed participates in, and while I do not condone you doing it, I also realize everyone has their journey to live. Be mindful of your environment and recognize a room full of blasted people isn't as safe as you think.

You are probably new to the effects of alcohol. Your desire to be able to say "Been there, done that" will override your critical thinking skills, and you will probably bong many a beer, shoot many a shot, and smoke plenty as well.

I speak a lot about drinking habits and how they can permeate throughout your life. I started this whole *College Success Habits* podcast, book, and speaking career with one of the goals being to help college students navigate the pressures vices will heave upon them.

As you focus more on your emotional maturation and development, it is my hope you see your negative habits and nip them out before you wake up as a forty-year-old who has no other option but to enter into sobriety.

Make no mistake—getting sober was the best decision I've ever made, over graduating from college and everything else. Perhaps if someone had told me how my habits would become lifelong residents in my life, I would've taken my habit making processes more seriously when I was eighteen to twenty-five.

A routine is a habit, and a habit is a routine. **Your identity is grounded in what you repeatedly do.** Therefore, build positive habits around everything you do. Be mindful and self-aware when building your routines/habits.

If you get a bad grade on a test, which leads you to the bar where you have a drunken blast with your friends, your brain is going to associate the two together. These not so subtle cues established in your life become the foundations for your unconscious behaviors.

Get a crappy grade . . . get drunk . . . have fun. The brain sees that getting bad grades leads to fun, so it doesn't get on board when you want to study, because that's not the trigger for fun—bad grades are.

Discipline can lose out to deeply habituated behaviors.

"Screw it! FOMO! YOLO! Let's go . . . eat, drink, be merry!" Whatever the action is can easily become the go-to response. The brain loves auto-pilot. It uses less energy, requires less concentration, and the reward is predetermined.

Of course, the reward for a hard night out is an even harder morning in, but only you'll know if the aftereffects of enjoying the drinking, sweets, or hours of streaming is enough to get you to create a new, more positive habit.

4. Are you mindful and self-aware? So you have your vision, you know your why, and you've built a powerful, positive feedback loop around the new habit/routine, so discipline is automatic.

Now, are you paying attention to your actions?

If you have ever gone into "trance" mode and mindlessly gone into autopilot, you are not alone; we have all done that.

And you'll do it many times over in your life, so don't be hard on yourself when it occurs. Just remind yourself that you are changing these behaviors and adjust your mindset into a positive state that is uplifting and not negatively degrading.

Ways to be more self-aware include meditation, self-reflection, and journaling. There are countless blogs and Google pages about this, so I won't delve into all of that. You can research those options on your own if they sound compelling.

In my own way, I do all three. I am regularly writing, recording podcasts and audio memos, practicing yoga, meditating, and self-reflecting about my decisions and their outcomes. Keep in mind, the outcomes are my responsibility to accept because they came from my actions.

One of my keys to self-awareness and mindfulness is staying present in the moment and pushing through those times when my brain wants to go off into daydream-land.

I love to daydream. I wish it were a profession. I don't actually want to create anything from my daydreams. I just want to live in my head and play around with my visions. Science doesn't have to exist there. I can defy gravity, teleport, bears can talk, bees invite me into their hive—it's nonstop hilarity and chaos in there.

I love it.

But gazing off into space and letting my mind have its fun

doesn't get anything accomplished in the real world. It can leave me tranced out, unmindful, and easily tempted by external forces I've set about eliminating from my life.

Drinking, drugs, sugar, porn, gambling, social media—all of these can trance you out, and when your brain is on autopilot, it's going to want more of the same, minute after minute, day after day.

Bummer of the day is that the more you give into those vices, the more of them you need each time to accomplish the same high, which isn't realistic because addiction and vices are depreciating assets. It will never be the same as the first time, and so on. Not without even more and more and more. . . . It'll slowly decline until you are freebasing Oreos and gambling away your car just to get that adrenaline rush again, even if for a brief moment.

Be self-aware.

Be mindful.

Don't freebase Oreos.

Don't freebase anything.

Ever.

Seriously—ever.

5. Are you consistently stressing yourself out? Stress is a son-of-a-bitch. It'll show up, set up camp, and not even pay rent. It'll drive you mad, hurt your body, and ultimately leave you feeling like no matter what you do; it was less than your best.

Have you ever finished an argument and thought you deserved some booze or sugar?

Have you left an exam and thought, "Yeah, that was stressful; I deserve some fried foods."

Stress triggers an emotion in us that generally leads to a compensating action.

- That was hard, I deserve this.

- That was a pain in the ass, I deserve this.
- That was stressful, I deserve a reward.

Willpower can be built up; it is a renewable resource, but it can be exhausted. It has to have time to renew. You need to cultivate positive habits in your life so your willpower isn't regularly depleted.

Stress uses willpower as fuel. Stress uses your intestinal fortitude as its nitric oxide to boost you to accomplish feats under tremendous pressure. This is good for acting under pressure, but again, you cannot always be calling upon willpower when stressed.

Have you ever said, "I get my best work done on a deadline"?

Aren't you just getting the work done because it is due soon? Waiting till the paper is due in six hours doesn't mean it's your best work, regardless of the grade you receive. It just means you got the job done and you earned the grade you earned.

Sure you got an A, but did you learn the material in a way that you'll be able to reflect upon it in the future and use it conversationally if the need arises?

If you're stressed because of an impending exam, studies show that you will increase your caffeine and/or nicotine consumption. Throw sugary and salty foods in there too. A dash of booze, or a guzzle, and you've got a great mixture of stress-increasing ingredients, not stress-reducing.

Stress is an inherent part of our lives, and to think you can eliminate it from your life is ridiculous. It can push you to great achievements if appropriately used, but allowing it to break your discipline or alter a positive habit is counterintuitive to building the best you.

When you slip—and you will—ease up on yourself and don't dive headfirst into self-defeating guilt. That would be like slipping up and eating an Oreo and then beating yourself up about it so you shrug your shoulders and say, "Well, I've already had one; I might as well eat the whole bag."

"I already took a shot, might as well drink the whole bottle."

What are your answers to stress?

- Meditating
- Taking a walk (preferably around trees and nature)
- Socializing
- Working out
- Physical activity
- Reading for pleasure (i.e., not for learning)

Whatever you use, anchor a habit around it. Do not just think stress will go away on its own. It sets up camp and stays. It might dissipate a bit, or recede for a while, but it knows how to come back with a vengeance. If you aren't set up to handle it in a healthy manner, you are going to be fighting it when you are maxed-out on bandwidth and most susceptible to turning toward a vice to help you through the overwhelm.

6. Who is in your circle of influence? Your social network can do wonders in elevating stress, or it can cause more of it.

The great Jim Rohn frequently said that we are the average of the five people we spend the most time with. If you want to get healthy, get in shape, and workout, but your closest five people eat out all the time, don't know where the campus gym is, and they'd rather binge-watch Netflix than take a walk and converse, how easy do you think it's going to be for you to stay disciplined on your new path?

When I quit drinking, I had to change the friends I was hanging around with. Fortunately for me, by the time I quit drinking, I had isolated myself so much that there weren't that many friends to cull from the herd—drinkers or otherwise.

At UF, when I decided to drink less and work out more, I found myself at home most nights. I didn't have the discipline to go out, be around drinkers, and not partake, so I stayed in.

Maybe you have the discipline to go out to eat with cheeseburger- and cheesecake-eating friends and still eat chicken and greens for dinner. Maybe you can go to the bar and drink soda or plain water, be social, and still have fun.

Whatever your threshold for abstinence when you're around your friends, only you can determine if you're capable of not changing your inner circle when you decide to better your habits.

Does your inner circle encourage you?

Do they push you to step outside your comfort zone?

Do they encourage you to try new things?

Do they motivate you to grow and become the best version of yourself?

Or do they do the opposite of these things?

Do you have parents who try to "bring you back to earth" when you have an idea? Friends who tell you to "reel in" your newest genius plan? Teachers who tell you that you can't accomplish something because it's predominantly a man's or woman's field?

I usually don't tell people what I am working on or my next great idea because I don't want to invite their opinions or advice into what I am doing. I wait until I have made some headway into the project, because giving my energy to others provides them with an opportunity to throw their point of view into the ring. If their POV comes from a fixed mindset, then their advice isn't going to gel with my growth mindset very well.

Choose your inner circle wisely. Be the positive influence your friends and family deserve to have around them. Then when you ask for the same positivity in return, the habit of support is already in place.

BE DISCIPLINED

Self-discipline begins with the mastery of your thoughts. If you don't control what you think, you can't control what you do.

NAPOLEON HILL

What If . . .

So you have everything in place, but you still find yourself undisciplined. Are you sure you have everything in place then?

Have you envisioned your vision?

Have you recognized your deep, deep why—not just the shallow response to why?

Have you set a clear plan?

Have you acknowledged your weakest areas and devised a plan to strengthen them?

Remove temptation. Want to eat healthier? Don't keep sugar in your home. Want to drink less or stop altogether? Don't keep booze in your house and ask your roommates to help you with that by keeping their booze out of the common areas.

Change your mindset around willpower. If you believe you have the willpower to resist temptation and stay disciplined, then you will. This is a fact. Realize that discipline builds up and strengthens. Having discipline in one area of your life will spill over to other areas of your life; it just takes time and patience. Understand the more prominent the temptation, the more discipline and willpower it will take to fend it off.

Have you rewarded yourself? When you follow through with a commitment and show yourself you can do whatever it is you asked of yourself, is the reward strong enough to cement that habit into place? When you let yourself down, forgive yourself, and renew your commitment to your integrity by following through the next time. Don't beat yourself up, because shaming yourself isn't healthy in the slightest.

Have you embraced forgiveness? You do not forgive others for them, but rather for you and your peace of mind. However, you do forgive yourself for yourself. No one else can give you that gift. If you slip up, forgive yourself, figure out why you slipped, and devise a new plan for the future when that temptation arrives again—and it will, count on it.

You don't have to be smarter than the rest; you have to be more disciplined than the rest.
WARREN BUFFETT

Summary

Cue → Craving → Response → Reward

Also known as:

Cue → Response → Reward

- Commit this to memory; this is how you build your habits, all your habits—both positive and negative, good and bad, powerful and weak.
- A routine is a habit, and a habit is a routine. **Your identity is grounded in what you repeatedly do.** Therefore, build positive habits around everything you do. Be mindful and self-aware when building your routines/habits.
- Stress triggers an emotion in us that usually leads to a compensating action.
- Willpower can be built up; it is a renewable resource, but it can be exhausted. It has to have time to renew. You need to cultivate positive habits in your life, so your

willpower isn't regularly depleted.

- Stress uses willpower as fuel. Stress uses your intestinal fortitude as its nitric oxide to boost you to accomplish feats under tremendous pressure. This is good for acting under pressure, but you cannot always be calling upon willpower when stressed; eventually you will run out and crack.

- Stress is an inherent part of our life. It can push you to great achievements if appropriately used but allowing it to break your discipline or alter a positive habit is counterintuitive to building the best you.

- Giving your energy to others provides them an opportunity to throw their opinion into the ring, so be wise about with whom you share your hopes, dreams, and ambitions.

Action steps to work through and follow. Write these down and go through them regularly.

- What is your vision?
- What is your "why?" (Know your deep, deep why, not just the shallow response to why.)
- Build a habit around it.
- Are you mindful and self-aware?
- Are you consistently stressing yourself out?
- Review who is in your circle of influence and decide if they are a positive influence.

Questions to ask yourself, work through, and follow. Write these down and go through them regularly.

- What is my way of dealing with stress?
- What is my clear plan?
- What are my weak areas?
- What is my plan to strengthen these areas?
- Is my inner circle a positive influence on me?
- How am I valuing my time?
- How do I value others and their time?

Important:

- What does *self-discipline* mean to me?
- Am I self-disciplined?
- Am I happy with the amount of self-discipline I have?

The more disciplined you become, the easier life gets.
STEVE PAVLINA

CHAPTER 6

EXERCISE FLEXIBILITY

Flexibility: *noun; the quality of bending easily without breaking; the ability to be easily modified; the willingness to change or compromise*

Why Is Flexibility Necessary?

I've never had anything in my life go 100 percent according to plan.

Plans are worthless, but planning is priceless.

It's a fact.

Google it.

Life comes at you rapidly. So much so that you can't possibly forsee what will come up as your task, project, paper, semester, year, or life unfolds.

Flexibility is critical because through that pliability you will better overcome challenges, reduce your stress level (when things do go awry), and ultimately be more successful than others who are more rigid and set in their ways.

When you are flexible, you have a distinct advantage over people who are less adept at adapting.

Your effectiveness in seeing infinite ways to arrive at your outcome will provide you with the confidence to take on any and all assignments, positions, and opportunities that come your way in school AND life.

You entered college with a plan and strategy. You are on a mission to grow as a human being so you can enter the workforce and earn the lifestyle you have desired ever since you knew what a lifestyle was.

Remember the growth mindset versus the fixed mindset? A growth mindset will help you figure out what to do when the plan goes bust. Flexibility and growth mindset are like twins; they are together all the time.

Accept these things to be true from here on out:

- Change is inevitable.
- You will have to pivot from your original idea.
- College is but a small part of your life, but it will have a far-reaching impact on your life's journey.

You've decided on your college. You've decided on your major. You've decided on where you're going to live. You've made a plethora of decisions on your way to that first class.

Take your shot.

You're in college.

Now, some of these decisions are less flexible:

- What university you're going to attend
- Where you're going to live
- Your roommate situation

These are presumably concrete for at least a year.

And some of them are more flexible.

Your major classes, diet, exercise routine, organizations to join, extracurricular activities to participate in, intramurals to play—all of these have varying ranges of fluidity.

It's essential to have a vision for your life, why you're in college, the career you want when you graduate—but you have to be flexible in how you'll get there.

I'll never forget the journalism story I was asked to write in third grade. I fell in love with journalism through that assignment and decided right then I wanted to be a journalist. I wanted to tell stories. I wanted to travel to find the stories. I wanted to see the world in my quest to find everything interesting.

Flash-forward to Ball State University in 1994. I wanted to be the next Bob Costas. I went to Ball State because their most famous alumnus, David Letterman, had donated lavishly to the telecommunications college. The building and the equipment were way ahead of the times, and it's even better now.

I planned to learn how to put together news stories, gain experience at the college TV station, and graduate to ESPN's Bristol's headquarters.

Instead, I passively deviated from my plan and became a party animal—aka, a drunk.

I don't remember looking in the mirror and saying, "Today you become an addict," but my behavior certainly seemed resolved to this new path.

That journey veered me wildly off course, but I never lost the sight of wanting to be a journalist.

After my junior year (shout-out to my .2 GPA that spring semester,) I dropped out of BSU and moved to Orlando in hopes that I'd get my head out of my ass.

When I started taking classes at Valencia Community College, I joined the school newspaper, eventually became the photo editor, and hesitantly wrote a couple of articles.

I wasn't the best writer then, and I'm still not, but photos I could take. I've had a passion for photography since my seventh birthday when my mom got me a camera. Unlike today, cameras were a big deal back then. We had to buy film *and* get them printed.

Throughout my time at VCC, I ran everything I did through my "become a journalist" filter. Once I graduated from Valencia, it was on to the University of Florida and the College of Journalism in Weimer Hall.

I must have changed my major's concentration a handful of times because I took writing, editing, photography, design, advertising, marketing, and magazine management classes galore. I didn't want to leave. I loved college so much—well, mostly the bartending and drinking every night, but there was enough school time to maintain a 3.0 GPA.

Working at UF's student newspaper, pursuing photography, learning how to design news pages all were done because of that third-grader's vision of becoming a journalist.

I was a jack-of-all-trades in college because I saw industry-changing trends in the internet's power. Remember, I started college in '94, when email was a black screen with green text, and by the time I graduated in 2006, Facebook, Twitter, and MySpace were just starting to make a name for themselves. I know, I know—MySpace. I just aged myself.

Side note: Not that it's important to this book, but I think the reason MySpace failed was that it gave the user too many options. You could change the code and make your page look any way you wanted. That was just too much freedom and too many choices for most people. The **paradox of choice** strikes again!

My first job out of school, as I mentioned, was working for a Dutch publisher, developing tabloids about investment opportunities in countries around the world. I lived, worked, and visited fifteen countries in 2008. My vision of being a journalist still held steady, but I was very flexible in how that looked and felt.

When I left that job and moved to Los Angeles, I had this headstrong notion that I was going to become a stand-up comedian, host a TV show, become famous, and through that get to host an environmentally based travel show. Improv and sketch comedy led to red-carpet reporting, which led to a web series, which led to a lead news anchor spot on a weekly talk show, which led to a sports reporting gig, which led to podcasting—and the list goes on.

In 2012, I spent the summer riding my '97 Honda Shadow motorcycle around the country, shooting the whole experience documentary-style. Twenty-nine states, 12,500 miles—from coast to coast and damn near from border to border.

I tell you all of this because I never stopped running my actions through the filter of becoming a journalist; I was just super flexible in my approach and plan. If I had locked myself into being a print or TV journalist, I could have easily overlooked the foreign and LA opportunities.

Today, I host multiple podcasts and give keynote speeches on topics like the ones I'm covering in this book. I teach workshops, host seminars, and retreats all because of that third-grader's vision of telling remarkable stories and my current ability to be flexible in the journey.

So be flexible in how you approach what you are passionate about and want to do for the rest of your life, or you will miss out on fantastic experiences.

Want to make God laugh? Tell him your plans.
WOODY ALLEN

What Is Flexibility?

Flexibility is the ability to demonstrate a fluid approach to your work, relationships, and life. It is being able to figure out a new way when an obstacle presents itself.

A detour does not ruin the trip. It provides you a chance to see something unexpected and perhaps even live a better story. Inflexible people get flustered quickly, complain often, and give up frequently. Giving up is what amateurs do—but you're not an amateur, right?

When working with other students and co-workers, your flexibility will provide them with confidence in your abilities. They will feel self-assured that you can handle unexpected situations with calm, ease, and certainty.

Being able to pivot and figure out different ways to do things isn't generally listed on one's resume—but it should be. You should feel confident in putting all seven of these principles on your resume as Jedi-level mastery.

Flexibility isn't just seeing life as ever-changing and evolving; it's doing things with an ever-changing and evolving attitude and work ethic.

I used to think college did little to prepare me for the real world. Then I got older, sober, and realized that everything I accomplished at BSU, VCC, and UF was in preparation for the life I lead now.

When you leave college, you will need to learn new programs, work manuals, skills, and the like—count on that. Along the way, you might even utter the phrase "College did not prepare me for this."

But didn't it?

Flexibility is just one skill I grew in college, yet it's one of the most beneficial to my overall happiness, and that has helped me tremendously in all my endeavors.

Didn't school allow you to expand your thinking, get along with diverse people, and learn in a mind-expanding environment?

College is a collection of people wanting to learn new things every day so their life is well-positioned in the future. It propagates the freedom to learn, grow, teach, lead, and experience life in a way you will likely not find anywhere else.

You might work at a company with similar traits to college; you might get involved with an organization like that, too, but as a collective unit, you will not find such a population-dense area of people uplifting their lives as you will in college.

Flexibility is being able to adapt to the college environment with enthusiasm and curiosity.

You do not know everything.

You have not experienced everything.

You haven't even begun to understand all of this.

You will look back, one day, and say, "If only I knew then what I know now."

It's a fact.

Google it.

Every human on this planet has said that in their life. Take this opportunity and do the most with it—learn, adapt, and grow, so you are more knowledgeable and flexible tomorrow.

> *Life is what happens while you are busy making plans.*
> JOHN LENNON

How to Be More Flexible

Ask yourself: "Is this a priority for me?" Knowing that answer will provide you with a good gauge on how flexible you need or want to be regarding the situation. I mean, you need to be flexible no matter what—but how are you going to be flexible?

When I decided to buy my first "new" car, my mind was set on a Hyundai Santa Fe. My dad and brother both owned one, and they spoke highly of it.

In my search for the best one for me, different years, colors, and options kept showing themselves. I *needed* a new car immediately because my Saturn's brakes were shot, and I couldn't drive it much longer without charging into the back end of the vehicle in front of me.

I had this crazy daydream in my head that the news choppers would be hovering above me on the highway as cops chased me, and the storyline was, "Saturn lunatic plowing through traffic in maddening road rage."

While there are plausible parts of that storyline, like me going mad because of the traffic, I did not want that scenario to be the first 400 links when you searched my name. As the only Jesse Mogle on the planet, I could not let "lunatic mad man" be the first thing you read about me on Google.

The hunt for the best Santa Fe, for me, proved daunting. Choosing how to be flexible during this car buying experience was essential to my prolonged happiness with my eventual new car.

I decided I would be flexible with the color, year, and miles, but I would not be flexible on some of the car's options, and of course, the make or model. I was going to own a Hyundai Santa Fe. It was going to have those lights on the side mirrors and make the beeping sound when someone was in my blind spot. It was going to have navigation and most importantly, a port for my iPhone so I could listen to audiobooks, podcasts, and iTunes.

Knowing my priorities on the features set the parameter for which crossover was acceptable and those that weren't. This, in turn, accurately set my flexibility meter so I could search with ease and confidence.

No stress. No worries. Just a fun monthlong journey till I found the right fit for me. Sure, it was in Orange County, a two-hour drive to the car lot with heavy traffic, but well worth it because the Santa Fe I found met my priorities entirely.

Action steps to work on and follow. Write these down and go through them regularly.

1. Start small, end big. Are you inflexible about little things in your life?

Where to eat?

Where the coffeepot is kept in the kitchen?

What kind of toothpaste to use?

If not, start there.

Flexibility will seep into your entire life if you use it with trivial decisions.

How will you manage your emotions when you discover your "must-have" class is full if you've already lost your temper over the coffeepot this morning?

2. Figure out your priority level for the intended outcome. Ask yourself, "What is my priority here, and what is my intended outcome for this situation?"

If you don't really care where you eat, then don't argue pizza to death when you could easily eat something else.

If pizza is a must, but your favorite place is closed or three hours back home, be flexible in finding a comparable location.

Knowing the priority level, like with my car's features, is super important in determining your mental and emotional energetic output in any situation. Don't freak out over something trivial. Take a breath. It'll be OK. There are other options for every scenario.

3. Stop, think, evaluate, move: STEM. STEM is a useful acronym for working through *any* issue. It's in this thinking that you'll embrace flexibility.

If the street to your favorite pizza place is closed, **stop** and **think** about other ways to get there.

Now do that with every situation in your life.

Your computer blacks out. Go to the library and work on their computers.

An interview falls through for a story. Call around till you find a suitable replacement.

Evaluate the options you have with a flexible mind, make a decision, and move on it. The longer you wait, the more you'll question your judgment.

Be thoughtful in your new decision and flexible in the issue's resolution. It may not turn out to be the best response, but it's in that action you will learn something that will help you in the future.

Additionally, we covered the **Move** portion of this acronym in the Action, Courage, and Decisiveness chapters.

All seven of these principles work together, in tandem, to help you produce the best possible outcome with the knowledge and resources you have at that time.

You will grow and learn, and with this newer version of yourself, you'll be able to make better and more educated decisions on how to proceed in the future.

The key here is to think about what you are doing, then ask yourself "Why am I doing this?"

WHY is *soooo* important I should make it a 42-sized font.

4. Alter your habits. I speak extensively on habits. This book and my podcast aren't called *College Success Habits* by accident.

If your morning routine goes in the same order every day without fail, shuffle brushing your teeth, washing your face, and showering. Try to alter the order. How easy is it for you to do? That's generally a good indicator of your overall flexibility.

Now change something up in your study habits. Add something new that you think will be helpful—perhaps a new location?

Altering your habits is a great way to test your flexibility.

Habits are unconscious processes you have grown accustomed to accomplishing with little thought.

Pulling that habit into the conscious part of your brain will be a fun little exercise to gauge your flexibility level.

5. Try something new. Perhaps you have a set grocery list you cook with, a set recipe you use for your favorite dish, or a favorite coffee brand.

Try something new. The worst thing that can happen is that one meal tastes crappy. One cup of coffee is botched.

It's not the end of the world. There are other meals—other cups of coffee.

Stepping out of the typical or traditional way you do things is an excellent way to experience life. Get into that habit.

6. Release the stress. You want to be flexible; I think we can agree on that by now. In your flexibility, you know you will have other choices to make in the future. Knowing, down the road, you can choose a different option or way of doing something that will reduce your decision-making stress.

Flexibility reduces stress . . . period. You know you can change things up in the future. Accept this, act on it, and evaluate as you go. Evaluating should be a constant while you're in action mode, and it's is a great habit to get into.

7. Trust yourself. Your life is a giant experiment. Trust that you will learn from each experience. Trust that these life experiences will come in handy down the road.

If you don't trust yourself, you will stay in your comfort zone, and that leads to minimal growth and lackluster enjoyment.

Plans are worthless, but planning is priceless.
THOM RIGSBY

What if . . .

If you find yourself inflexible, then run yourself through the above list and ask yourself why you aren't embodying those traits.

You can "what if" your life to death.

The truth is:

No matter how many scenarios you think up . . .

No matter how many questions you ask . . .

No matter how many answers I give . . .

You cannot prepare for every scenario.

But Jesse (whiny voice):

What if I'm not flexible?

What if there isn't anything to eat and I'm hungry?

What if there isn't any coffee?

What if I'm tired?

What if I can't pay a bill on time?

What if I can't study because I have to work?

If you're not flexible, it's because you're choosing not to be.

Think up different ways you can get some food in your belly ("borrowing" your roommate's peanut butter and bread perhaps.)

Do some jumping jacks instead of drinking coffee.

Call the billing company and see if they can extend your due date or set up a payment plan.

There is time to work and study—figuring out how is where flexibility and the growth mindset are hanging out.

The "what if's" come from an inflexible mind, and that's the world of an amateur.

No matter what I write here, I couldn't possibly cover every "what if" you conjure up. So stop asking what if and start thinking *I'll figure it out*.

Every solution is just one STEM away.

> *Stay committed to your decisions,*
> *but stay flexible to your approach.*
> TONY ROBBINS

Summary

- **Nothing ever goes 100 percent according to plan.**

- Flexibility is the ability to demonstrate a fluid approach to your work, relationships, and life. It is being able to figure out a new way when an obstacle shows itself.

- Flexibility is critical because through that pliability you will better overcome challenges, reduce your stress level (when things do go awry), and ultimately be more successful than others who are more rigid and set in their ways.

- Your effectiveness in seeing infinite ways to arrive at your outcome will provide you with the confidence to take on any and all assignments, positions, and opportunities that come your way in school *and* beyond.

- Remember that a growth mindset will help you figure out what to do when a plan goes bust. Flexibility and a growth mindset are like twins—they are together all the time.

- Accept these things to be true from here on out:

  - Change is inevitable.

  - You will have to pivot from your original idea.

  - Time wise, the college experience is a relatively brief portion of your life, but its impact on your life's journey will be remarkably far-reaching.

- Be flexible in how you approach what you are passionate about and want to do for the rest of your life, or you will miss out on fantastic experiences.

Action steps to work through and follow. Write these down and go through them regularly.

- Start small; end big. Are you making too big a deal over small decisions like lattes and sock color?
- Figure out your priority level for the intended outcome.
- Stop, think, evaluate, move: STEM.
- Alter your habits.
- Try something new.
- Release the stress
- Trust yourself.

Questions to ask yourself, work through, and follow. Write these down and go through them regularly.

- Am I inflexible in my small decisions?
- Am I selfish?
- Am I setting healthy boundaries?
- Where can I compromise?
- What is my priority level for this?
- Where can I alter a habit to make it more positive?
- Do I trust myself?

Important:

- Am I using **STEM?**

CHAPTER 7

EMBODY TENACIOUSNESS

Tenacity: noun; the quality or act of being very determined; the quality of being tenacious or of holding fast; persistence.

Why Is Tenaciousness Important?

It's real simple. You have to show up every day. Every single day you have to be present in your own life. **It's so important to show up physically, emotionally, mentally, and spiritually** (don't get locked on that word and think religion—it's more about morals, ethics, and values) **in your life that putting this in bold, italics, and a font of 117 still wouldn't do it justice.**

Choose to show up every day as the best version of yourself. Your attitude, mentality, emotional state are all choices you get to make every moment of every day.

For you, being tenacious in college means doing as I say now, not as I did then.

I drank my face off in college. From age eighteen to thirty, my primary focus was inebriation. Yes, I accomplished a lot of stuff. My formula for success was using these seven principles when my back was to the wall.

I don't want your back against a wall. I don't want you looking

93

up at a cliff's face wondering how you got there and how you are going to scale it.

Just by being here and reading this book, you are already in a better position than half your classmates—and certainly better than I was.

If you genuinely care about yourself, the opportunities offered to you, your college journey, and your life, you will get yourself out of bed, get yourself together, and be ready for anything and everything.

Some keys to remember and thrive through:

- Be where you say you're going to be when you say you're going to be there.
- Don't change the way you act to impress others.
- Don't hide behind the shy armor.
- Don't keep your hand down because you're afraid of the outcome.
- Don't be a person you will reflect upon one day and regret being.
- Be the best version of yourself today.
- Strive each morning to be better than you were the day before.

Tenacity is a crucial personality trait because there are going to be so many different hurdles, barriers, and boundaries in your way—in college and throughout your life.

There is going to be friction.

There will be imbalances you have to overcome.

There will be plenty of opportunities for you to quit because of adversity.

I can promise you all of this and more.

The worst-case scenario is missing out on the best-case scenario.

I shudder to think how many times I allowed myself to stay home, stay on the couch or in bed, drink away my feelings, and just let life pass by me.

Taking the six guiding principles we've already covered into account, tenacity is the one that ensures you push forward and continue the positive feedback loop of going through the previous six—in every aspect of your life.

Developing a growth mindset means you realize that your mind is what limits you, and you are the boss in there, not the other way around. You control your thoughts; don't let them control you.

To **cultivate courage**, you have to move through your fears and continue forward - even when your thoughts are pushing to keep you safe and in your comfort zone. **Sometimes you have to do it afraid.**

Being decisive requires you to make a decision and be confident in it. Do not question yourself. You made your selection—now move!

Taking action is showing up and getting to it. It's literally that easy. Just do it!

Embracing discipline is being committed to yourself and your decisions. Hold yourself accountable and show up 100 percent when you commit.

Exercising flexibility is understanding there are infinite possibilities in this universe, and when a hurdle approaches, you know you'll figure it out.

Tenacity shows itself in all of the above. Every one of these principles requires you to show up, be present, and be your best self.

How you do anything is how you do everything.
ZEN BUDDISM (ACCORDING TO SIMON SINEK)

What Is Tenacity?

Tenacity is trying different approaches, to achieving a goal, until you find the one that works best for you. (Notice how flexibility plays a role here too.)

According to the dictionary definition, tenacity is "the quality or fact of being very determined."

Well, that's easy enough. Being determined is being tenacious.

Be determined to show up, experience it, and do it all with a growth-mindset.

Google says *tenacity* is "the state of holding on to an idea or a thing very strongly."

And you can do that because you've already run your decision through the previous six principles to ensure you are congruent with your choice.

Have the growth mindset to know if you keep showing up, good things will happen. You might hate your job, but if you show up every day, you're gonna get paid—and getting paid is better than eating ramen noodles three times a day.

You might not like a class, but you have to go anyway. If you study your butt off, work diligently, and ask the professor questions you need answers to, you will either succeed or you'll figure out why you're not.

If you are determined to play half-assed, to arrive with a hangover, half asleep, and otherwise disheveled, your experience will mirror that, and you will only have yourself to blame for the outcome.

Since *tenacity* is "the quality displayed by someone who just won't quit until the goal is reached," there's something you need to figure out about yourself.

Do you recognize when something is no longer serving you?

There are important differences in being tenacious versus self-care mindful. We'll go more in-depth in the "What if . . ." section, but don't go skipping ahead. Be determined to finish this chapter in the order I wrote it or at least be flexible enough to skip ahead and come back—it's your choice; you're in charge here.

> *You can't turn work ethic off and on like a light switch.*
> *You either have it, or you don't.*
> JESSE MOGLE

How to Be Tenacious

I've shared two of my favorite quotes in this chapter:

> *How you do anything is how you do everything.*

> *You can't turn work ethic off and on like a light switch.*
> *You either have it, or you don't.*

To me, these two quotes are the essence of tenacity. You become this—you encapsulate this as a foundational aspect of your personality—and the world will be calling you boss one day.

How do you encompass tenacity?

Here's my action step loop for tenacity:

1. Know your why, envision your vision, and determine the outcome you want to achieve.

2. Have flexibility in your approach.

3. Pay attention to the journey as it unfolds.

4. Learn from each step along the way.

5. Evaluate your purpose in going through this experience.

6. Be nonjudgmental in the way you connect your

experiences and point of view to someone else's experiences and point of view.

7. Build a trustworthy social circle that supports you in this endeavor.

8. Re-evaluate your purpose, the benefits, the vision, and your intended outcome regularly.

Move forward with this renewed perspective and this list regularly.

For me, the key to maintaining my tenacious drive toward my passions, tasks, goals, outcomes, and visions is consistent self-awareness of how my daily actions are affecting this loop.

It's easy to become overwhelmed in college, go into survival mode, and overlook what is going on around you.

You will have fifty things happening in one day. You will have multiple assignments with the same due date. You will have a shift at your job on that same day. You will have exams, roommate conflicts, friend issues—everything and more will fall on your plate at the same time.

When you step back, evaluate what's happening, list them so you know what's immediate versus further off, and figure out what you can get off your desktop right now, you will have greater control. You will begin to see things are merely overwhelming you because you are choosing to let them overwhelm you.

Overwhelm is a perspective. If you shift your perspective, by evaluating what it is that is stressing you out, overwhelm will give way to clarity, confidence, and control.

You know how to get things done on time. The main problem is that, without the right planning, your to-do list can look insurmountable.

We both know the answer lies in being organized, being

committed to action, and being tenacious in your efforts to stay on track.

College is meant to test you because that's what life does best: it tests you. Remember saying, "I can't wait to be a grown-up so I can do whatever I want"? Well, here we are, in the land of the grown-ups. Some will pull it off better than you, and others will not. Please, hear this and take it to heart—you are not competing against them. You're competing against yesterday's version of yourself. Be better than that person.

Embody tenaciousness by purposefully following the previous six principles and push through the mess that will fall in your path. If you have the mindset that you'll overcome whatever presents itself to you, then you will achieve whatever you focus your mind on.

Many parents tell their kids:

You can be anyone you want to be.

You can do anything you want to do.

You can achieve whatever your heart desires.

The main problem is this part is often left out—**you are going to have to work your ass off for what you want in life.** You must show up every day, with your "getting shit done" hat on, and bust your rump until you accomplish your goals.

That's how you embody tenacity, and don't let anyone tell you otherwise.

No one is going to hand you the keys to the kingdom. No one is going to throw you the deed to their mansion and super yacht. You don't just wake up the CEO or on the best and brightest under twenty, thirty, or forty lists.

If someone comes to you and says you can half-ass your way to success, they are the enemy, and they don't want you to succeed. They see you as a threat, and their advice should be ignored in favor of your own thinking.

Repeat after me, "I will work as hard as I know I can, and I'll get the job done to the best of my abilities—every time."

What If . . .

What if you begin to see yourself falling away from a tenacious, "I will accomplish anything" attitude?

Ask yourself if you are perseverant, tenacious, or persistent.

Knowing the differences in these words will alert you to the approach you've been taking.

Perserverant is trying to do something over and over again without changing the approach. I've also heard this jokingly called the definition of insanity.

If you aren't changing your approach and the resulting output is the same each time, you are not tenacious—you are wasting your time. You are buffering away actual progress in favor of doing something you are already comfortable doing.

No actual growth comes from staying in your comfort zone.

Tenacity is when you try different approaches to achieving a goal until you find the one that works for you. We've been covering that.

Persistence is combining the two so you have maximum flexibility. Life is a giant experiment. Everything you try in life is an experiment.

Do you like it?

Does it serve you?

Do you want to continue to experience it in the future?

Sometimes the experiment is flawed. Sometimes repeating the same steps does provide a different outcome or, at the very least, further studies on what not to do.

Other times changing the approach is best, but the results are the same or similar. Then you get even more flexible and try something else. The most minor of tweaks can result in the most major of differences.

A pilot barely has to fly a plane today. Mostly, computers keep them on their intended path. My pilot friends tell me the most dangerous and challenging part of their job is the takeoff and landing.

But the pilot doesn't get up and walk around during the trip. They stay at the controls and keep the plane on its exact course. If the plane starts to veer off track by even one degree throughout a three thousand-mile flight, that can mean the difference between landing in New York City or Washington, D.C.

Look at your college life like flying a plane. The hardest parts are taking off and sticking the landing. You must get in motion to stay in motion—and finishing strong is equally important. No one wants to walk across the finish line—instead, you want to sprint to it and stomp on that damn line.

Get in the habit of starting strong and finishing strong.

I run 5 and 10Ks here and there, and when I do, I start fast, settle into a pace, and then sprint the finish.

And about the actual journey through college—one degree off and you end up hundreds of miles from where you intended. Keep adjusting yourself so you stay on course. Be flexible in your approach. Know when you are being persistent, tenacious, and/or perseverant.

Remember above when I brought up tenacity versus self-care topic?

There will be times when you'll have to quit things, let something go, because you've determined after careful thought that **it no longer serves you**. Whatever that thing is, it is doing you more harm than good.

Think back to a time when you had to decide to release something you once enjoyed. Can you remember an experience like that? Great! That means you're paying attention to your life.

If not, let me help. Think about a: relationship, friendship, job, after-school activity, book, article, social media app—the list is infinite. With reflection, you no doubt can think of at least ten things you said goodbye to because they were no longer serving you.

It's not quitting when you know that the activity is no longer serving your greater good and that continuing it would set you back in a counterproductive way.

But—and this is a big BUT—you can't just stop three steps into a thousand-step journey and say, "Well, I tried. It didn't work for me. I'm out!"

You had no clue what that journey was going to be like because you gave it a half-assed effort, so therefore you got a half-assed result.

There are a plethora of reasons why you might need to stop doing something, quit something, move on from something, and only you will know if that's a self-care decision you need to make or an excuse you're giving yourself to quit because it got hard.

Learning to play the guitar, let's say during the first ten lessons, isn't going to be comfortable as you practice bending your fingers around the neck, which might cause some wrist pain.

Yes, it is difficult. Then comes learning the chords, playing them in sequence, strumming at the right time, and so much more. If you have the determination to show up every single day, down the line, you will be able to play "Happy Birthday" for sure.

You will get better if you have a growth mindset that says, "I will figure this out."

Now, if those guitar lessons are at the same time as a class you need to take, a study session you must attend, whatever it is—you have to decide which to make a priority.

Re-prioritizing activities doesn't mean you are quitting.

It just means, right now, there is something else you'd rather prioritize.

It doesn't mean you won't try it again later.

Tenacity comes from being determined. Determination comes from being happy and confident about the priorities you placed into your life—the positive feedback loop in place.

If something different would better serve your college career, that year, that semester, that class, then know when to make the switch, be growth-oriented, be decisive, and get into action, so you get the most out of what you are doing.

Making a decision, then questioning it while you're doing it is a horrible thing to do to yourself.

Talk about a way to get out of alignment and congruency with yourself real quick.

Every single situation in your life is an opportunity to learn something new or improve an already existing skill.

A wise man and a fool meet upon a path who learns more?
The wise man—because a fool never listens.
AUTHOR UNKNOWN

Summary

- Tenacity is trying different approaches, to achieving a goal, until you find the one that works best for you. (Notice how flexibility plays a role here too.)

- **Show up physically, emotionally, mentally, and spiritually in your life.** Choose to show up every day as the best version of yourself. Your attitude, mentality, emotional state are all choices you get to make every moment of every day.

- If you genuinely care about yourself, the opportunities offered to you, your college journey, and your life, you will get your ass out of bed, get yourself together, and be ready for anything and everything.

Some keys to remember and thrive through:

- Be where you say you're going to be when you say you're going to be there.

- Don't change the way you act to impress others.

- Don't hide behind the shy armor.

- Don't keep your hand down because you're afraid of the outcome.

- Don't be a person you will reflect on one day and regret being.

- Be the best version of yourself today.

- Strive each morning to be better than you were the day before.

Action steps to work through and follow. Write these down and go through them regularly.

- Know your why, envision your vision, and determine the outcome you want to achieve.

- Have flexibility in your approach.

- Pay attention to the journey as it unfolds.

- Learn from each step along the way.

- Evaluate your purpose in going through this experience.

- Be nonjudgmental in the way you connect your experiences and point of view to someone else's experiences and point of view.

- Build a trustworthy social circle that supports you in this endeavor.

- Re-evaluate your purpose, the benefits, the vision, and your intended outcome regularly.

Move forward with this renewed perspective and this list regularly.

Questions to ask yourself, work through, and follow. Write these down and go through them regularly.

- Why do I want to pursue this goal? (Be honest with yourself here. Is it negative energy like greed, ego, pride, attention, etc. or positive energy like an accomplishment, being of service, financial security, etc.?)
- What's the best-case scenario if I achieve this goal?
- What's the worst-case scenario if I don't achieve this goal?
- Am I afraid of failure?
- Am I afraid of success?
- Am I acting through emotion rather than thoughtful consideration?
- What is the honest reason I am continuing or quitting?

Important:

- What advice would you give to someone in your position?

CONCLUSION

No! Hell No! What? Are you kidding me?

Abject anger at its best—but seriously, no, this is not the end of our journey together.

First and foremost, go to your preferred podcasting app and subscribe to College Success Habits, and check out ALL the episodes.

I reviewed each of these chapters in episodes eleven through eighteen. It's an audiobook of sorts, as I discuss the seven power principles you just finished reading.

The best thing about self-improvement and personal development is that it never ends; you might stop actively pursuing it, but you will forever be changing. The question is: Are you evolving? Accept change as inevitable. Growing is a part of life, but personal growth and development takes a concentrated effort.

This book is an outline for the powerful principles you need . . . check that, you must embody . . . to reach your life's highest fulfillment.

You cannot half-ass your way to your best life ever! Be focused on what it is you want in life, and you will achieve it—even if it doesn't look the way you thought it would when you first envisioned the outcome.

Develop a growth mindset; this will keep you in a state of confidence that you can learn anything new, become whatever you desire—because your skills, talents, and habits are always upgradeable.

Step into the courageousness life demands of you. **Cultivate courage** by accepting that life is a journey, and it rewards those who are willing to take the most risks.

Use your courage. **Be decisive**, and make a decision. Do not question yourself—you are a mindful person. You STEM-ed: Stopped, Thought, Evaluated, and Moved—so you know the choice you made was the best one for you at that time. Remember, questioning yourself the whole time isn't decisive—it's wishy-washy.

Being patient isn't the act of waiting; it's the attitude you have while waiting. In the same way, being decisive isn't the act of making a decision; it's the attitude of confidence you have during and after you make the decision that determines decisiveness.

Take action and move on the decision you made. You are "all about that action, boss," and that is why you will achieve what you want in college and life.

Embrace discipline because that is how you stick with the plan and get to an outcome. It may not be the outcome you thought it would be when you started, but it is an outcome either way—and now you can move on to the next project, task, or goal with the experience of completion under your belt and the faith in yourself that you do what you say you will do.

Exercise flexibility in your life. Know that rarely does anything go according to plan, and because you are flexible, you know you can bounce to the beat no matter how it plays out.

Embody tenaciousness because consistently showing up as the best version of yourself is the only way to accomplish what it is you want in life. In the book *The Four Agreements*, Don Miguel Ruiz states the fourth agreement as "Always be your best." You do this through tenacity; it's as simple as that.

CONCLUSION

What kind of learner are you?

You may have noticed that my chapters are laid out in a Why, What, How, What If format. There is a reason for this: these are four types of learning styles.

If you are a **Why learner,** you tend to need personal meaning as to why you are going to learn something. If the professor, or boss, can bridge that gap for you, then you are all in and will learn the new material readily. If you focus on why things are important and why things are the way they are by seeking clarity and meaning in new material, then you tend toward the Why learning style.

Questions you ask yourself or the instructor:

"Why do I need this?"

"Why is this important?"

"Why did you say that?"

If you are a **What learner,** you tend to focus on what there is to learn and the facts because facts lead to a deeper understanding of the subject. If you seek continuity and absolutes in the material, if you enjoy creative concepts, history, lectures, and the like, then you lean toward a What learning style.

Questions you ask yourself or the instructor:

"What is this all about?"

"What are the facts or specifics?"

"What do I need to know?"

If you are a **How learner,** you tend to focus on how things work. You like to get a real experience of the knowledge, and "try things on." If you seek usability, benefits, results, and enjoy the practical application of ideas and information, then How is probably your preferred learning style.

Questions you ask yourself or the instructor:

"How do I do it?"

"How does this work?"

"How can I use this in the future?"

If you are a **What if learner,** you tend to focus on how the new information can help better your possibilities, and you want to future pace all possible scenarios so you can be as prepared as possible for whatever is to come. If you seek hidden opportunities and like to think outside the box, then What If is probably your preferred style of learning.

Questions you will ask yourself or the instructor:

"What if this happens?"

"What if I did it this way?"

These are the four styles of how people learn. This isn't the definitive way ALL people learn, but these are the four main ways people use when learning new material.

Figure out which one you tend toward, and you will go miles with this knowledge of yourself. Trust me, discovering my learning style was a gem for me to find. I tend toward Why, What, and How. Depending on what I am learning, either of those three can be the most important to me. I am not a What If learner at all. There is only so much future pacing I want to deal with when I am learning.

I am more than fine figuring it out in the future. The exception: when I am driving through the desert—then I always think about the "what if" and carry many gallons of water in my trunk.

Please, above all else, don't freak out that you don't know how to do something right now. You will learn what it is you need to learn when the time to learn it arrives.

Something I have experienced over and over again in my speaking, teaching, podcasting, and coaching is this. People have an insatiable appetite for to-do lists and instructions on how to do any and everything.

So often, I mean like all the time, I see people get the information they just couldn't live without—and then walk away from it.

They will save the url on their computer, put the book on the shelf, and then go on their merry way, comfortable in their headspace, knowing they have the information waiting if they ever decide to use it.

In the industry, we call this "shelf-help."

Do Not let this book become SHELF-HELP!

You will succeed in life when you adopt a plan and stick with it. Every amazing athlete has a strategy for their physical development, and they work within that structure for years. Yes, they adopt new strategies as they age, and after years of doing their sport, the structure of their physical regimen probably looks nothing like it did when they were a teenager in high school.

But the key is that they make incremental changes over time and don't completely start a new when things aren't going as they would like.

Adopt this mindset. You don't need to blow-up your strategy or plan when things aren't developing the way you had envisioned. Make tweaks to your personal syllabus and monitor your new path for signs it will take you to the outcome you desire.

You've got this. You now have the Seven Powerful Principles you need to become the best version of yourself. You are officially ready to excel in college and beyond.

Go back, reread the sections you want to master or refamiliarize yourself with when doubts start to creep into your mind.

You are doing the best you can with the resources you have. Every day you will learn new things, realize new ideas, believe new beliefs, and become a new person.

I can't wait for you to become the best version of yourself.

I can't wait to hear how this book has helped you.

I can't wait for you to get older and say, "If only I knew then what I know now."

Hopefully, this book keeps you from saying it as often as I have.

I'll be waiting for you to get here. We can share some soda water together.

And that's all, folks . . . for now.

Want to continue your *College Success Habits* journey?
Go to your favorite podcasting app and search "College Success Habits" or "Jesse Mogle." Just because the book is over doesn't mean the conversation is.

CPSIA information can be obtained
at www.ICGtesting.com
Printed in the USA
LVHW052323280520
656872LV00019B/3044